Homecoming Queens

Social Fictions Series

Series Editor

Patricia Leavy
USA

International Editorial Advisory Board

Carl Bagley, *University of Durham, UK*
Anna Banks, *University of Idaho, USA*
Carolyn Ellis, *University of South Florida, USA*
Rita Irwin, *University of British Columbia, Canada*
J. Gary Knowles, *University of Toronto, Canada*
Laurel Richardson, *The Ohio State University (Emerita), USA*

Scope

The *Social Fictions* series emerges out of the arts-based research movement. The series includes full-length fiction books that are informed by social research but written in a literary/artistic form (novels, plays, and short story collections). Believing there is much to learn through fiction, the series only includes works written entirely in the literary medium adapted. Each book includes an academic introduction that explains the research and teaching that informs the book as well as how the book can be used in college courses. The books are underscored with social science or other scholarly perspectives and intended to be relevant to the lives of college students—to tap into important issues in the unique ways that artistic or literary forms can.

Please consult www.patricialeavy.com for submission requirements (click the book series tab).

Homecoming Queens

J. E. Sumerau

SENSE PUBLISHERS
ROTTERDAM/BOSTON/TAIPEI

A C.I.P. record for this book is available from the Library of Congress.

ISBN: 978-94-6351-207-7 (paperback)
ISBN: 978-94-6351-208-4 (hardback)
ISBN: 978-94-6351-209-1 (e-book)

Published by: Sense Publishers,
P.O. Box 21858,
3001 AW Rotterdam,
The Netherlands
https://www.sensepublishers.com/

All chapters in this book have undergone peer review.

Printed on acid-free paper

ADVANCE PRAISE FOR
HOMECOMING QUEENS

"*Homecoming Queens* is a fascinating window onto rural queer life. Through the experiences of the novel's protagonist, Jackson, a bisexual, polyamorous man who leaves Tampa to support his spouses in moving back to their hometown in rural Georgia to run a family business, Sumerau addresses complex issues related to identities, families, and relationships among people across a diverse range of gender identifications and sexual and relationship orientations. Grounded in extensive ethnographic research on religion, gender, and sexuality in the American South, *Homecoming Queens* presents an intimate, compelling depiction of how polyamorous people live and love."
– Brandy Simula, Ph.D., Emory University

"J.E. Sumerau is an incredibly gifted writer. By the end of *Homecoming Queens*, I felt as though I personally knew Jackson, Crystal, and Lee (the three main characters) because Sumerau wrote them in such a way that they seem unique (as bisexual poly folks) but like every other human in their emotions and desires. *Homecoming Queens* educates you about being queer, trans, and poly in the South while also entertaining you with a captivating story from start to finish. Seriously, this story should be turned into a play or movie – or both!"
– Eric Anthony Grollman, Ph.D., University of Richmond and Editor of Conditionallyaccepted.com

"*Homecoming Queens* immediately draws you into the lives of characters that are faced with decisions to make as both individuals and as part of a committed union. The past, present, and future come together to set in motion a page-turning story about what it means to go home and the homes and families people build along the way as they build lives that defy gender and sexuality binaries. The characters offer a down-to-earth and insightful perspective on the multiplicity of gender and sexual identities through their

relationships and interactions with one another, especially that of bisexuality and polyamory, often not centrally situated in academic or fictional writing. *Homecoming Queens* shows that while the past may sometimes reverberate into our present, it does not necessarily have to define our present or the futures we seek. This book will keep you guessing and wondering long after you've read it."
– Lorena Garcia, Ph.D., University of Illinois Chicago and author of *Respect Yourself, Protect Yourself: Latina Girls and Sexual Identity*

"*Homecoming Queens* is an intertwined, genuine, and hilarious story about love, compromise, and what it means to be unknowing-but willing-to follow love to wherever our *loves* can convince us to go. Sumerau is (somehow) brilliantly able to capture what it means to be *trying* for multiple people, while figuring out ourselves. Undoubtedly, this novel broadens our ideas about relationships, identity, and companionship, making us question our own boundaries and what we'd be willing to put on the line for the people we care for the most. In return, we start to recognize all of the ways in which others do the same for us. Heartfelt, genuine and just straight up fun, *Homecoming Queens* certainly, and deservedly so, takes the crown!"
– Brittany Harder, Ph.D., University of Tampa

"Witty, action-packed, and full of surprises, Sumerau's *Homecoming Queens* will speak to anyone who has ever tried to go home again. In a web of local color and southern charm, *Homecoming Queens* transports us from queer-friendly Tampa, Florida to the small, conservative town of Queens, Georgia – *hometown* to two of three spouses in a polyamorous relationship. Sumerau's novel is an eye-opening read that sheds light on the dynamics of polyamory and queer presence in the Deep South. Secrets and mysteries intertwine with friendships new and old as the three spouses navigate Queens as sexually non-conforming adults. When the past meets the present, rumors collide with truth and all hell breaks loose, but will Queens and her newest poly residents survive?"
– Katie Acosta, Ph.D., Georgia State University and author of *Amigas y Amantes: Sexually Nonconforming Latinas Negotiate Family*

"In this beautifully written novel, Sumerau illustrates the passion, heartache, joy, frustration, and sheer complexity of what it means to be in a loving, committed partnership, especially when that partnership does not fit the monogamous and heterosexual standards of American society. Moreover, *Homecoming Queens* is not just a story about Queer folks navigating relationships and life in the American South. It is a story about the compromises we make to love and to be loved in return. It is a story about the lessons we learn when we take the time to examine how our own lives – and the lives of those around us – overlap and intersect across time and place. After reading this novel, I am reminded of the struggles we face when we walk paths of most resistance; yet, I am also left with a sense of optimism about the often small but impactful footprints we leave as we walk along those paths. Whether you're interested in learning about people in Queer relationships or you're simply looking for a short but illuminating read, *Homecoming Queens* is sure to have just what you need."
– **Harry Barbee, M.S., Doctoral Candidate and Instructor at Florida State University**

"Sumerau's book captures the essence embodied in and through true relationships—starting right away through the 'hate' that can only come from love. Sumerau successfully offers insights into the core of relationships, no matter the package they may come in, through immediately drawing the reader in through the loving yet complex matters the book's trio must face. Through the conversational writing style, the book creates a welcoming environment where the reader connects with the narrator's (lack of) conundrum, as they enter down a life path they promised they never would, and yet within five minutes are swept away because of love—messages and accessible examples of love even more needed in the current social context. The book captures local details without distraction or feeling forced, helping to uplift the importance of space, place, and context to lived experience. As with classic novels, the timelessness that comes from the time and space-specific writing quickly transports the reader to a new place. The details help the reader to see the shared humanity of

hopes, dreams, and hobbies that drives each of us, no matter our age, sexuality, race, or career (or lack thereof). The book offers a bridge across stereotypes, relationships and places, along with another much-needed outlet to help people see the continued, if not increasing, power of words."
– Amanda Koontz, Ph.D., University of Central Florida

"J.E. Sumerau brings us another rich, complex, and hilarious novel about people navigating relationships, sexuality, and friendships in the deep South. Exploring bisexual, trans, and polyamorous experience along the way, *Homecoming Queens* feels both familiar and fresh as Sumerau unpacks the tensions between tradition and the transformative power of love. *Homecoming Queens* shines a light on the deep desire for and limits to community building across social divides and gifts us with characters who remind us that "home" can be as fluid as love."
– Katherine McCabe, M.A., Doctoral Candidate and Instructor at University of Illinois Chicago

Previous Novels by J. E. Sumerau

Cigarettes & Wine

Essence

To Lain, for so many reasons

TABLE OF CONTENTS

TABLE OF CONTENTS

PREFACE

"It's hard for me to keep a straight face at the thought of living in a place called Queens with my husband and former homecoming queen wife," Jackson thinks when his spouses inform him of their desire to move back to their hometown following the death of one of their parents. In *Homecoming Queens*, this death and decision set in motion a series of events that will dramatically transform the three spouses, their understanding of the past, and the town itself.

As lifelong city dweller Jackson Garner leaves behind his comfy life in Tampa, his "favorite" casual lover who visits every year to see him, and the first place he's ever felt at home, he introduces us to Queens, a small town in Georgia situated between Atlanta and Augusta. While the spouses – Jackson, Crystal and Lee – adjust to small town life, they encounter supportive regulars at the diner they take over from Crystal's father Chuck, hostile locals who find bisexuality, polyamory, and other "alternative" lifestyles unsavory, and the traumatic event that led Crystal and Lee to leave town after high school in the first place. Along the way, they encounter the history and ghosts of the town, the tension between an LGBT friendly pastor and some of his anti-LGBT congregants, the struggles of a teen seeking gender transition against the beliefs of their family, and the ongoing battle between progress and tradition in the American south. Through Jackson's eyes, we walk with the spouses as they navigate tensions about sexuality, gender, family, race, and religion brought to the surface by their arrival.

Although written as a first-person narrative that allows readers to imagine themselves in Jackson's situation and experience the town and tensions first hand with him, *Homecoming Queens* is a novel about relationships; the ways our past often shapes our present whether we notice it or not, and how the people we become often relies heavily upon the other people, places, narratives, and cultures we encounter. As in life, the ways individuals are intertwined within various relationships permeate the events captured in the following pages. *Homecoming Queens* offers a view into the ways various types of relationships and cultural norms play out in the experiences of a given romantic, geographic and familial context as well as the ways people adjust to unexpected events in the course of their lives. It also provides a first-person view of the ways families, hometowns, friends, lovers, spouses, local histories, places, religions, and broader social norms influence relationships.

Homecoming Queens also presents explorations of bisexual and poly relationships all too rarely available in contemporary media or academic materials. Alongside academic and media portrayals of the world that generally only focus on monosexual and monogramous options (i.e., what scholars call mononormativity), *Homecoming Queens* allows readers to imagine what such norms look like from the perspective of a bisexual, poly person as well as the ways Americans often react to these realities when they come into view. Especially at a time when these subjects are often difficult for even college professors to talk about and generally missing from social scientific scholarship, *Homecoming Queens* supplies readers with an opportunity to view the world, society, the American south, families, marriage, and small towns through a bisexual and poly lens. Readers seeking more information on these subjects may also want to check out, for example, https://bisexual.org/home/ for information on the bisexuality spectrum, and http://www.lovemore.com for information on poly sexualities and relationships.

While entirely fictional, *Homecoming Queens* is grounded in my own experience as a bisexual (on the pansexual end of the spectrum), genderqueer (formerly identified as a crossdresser and still considering potential transition), and historically poly person raised in the American south. It is also built upon years of ethnographic, auto-ethnographic, historical and statistical research I have done concerning intersections of sexualities, gender, religion, and health, and hundreds of formal and informal interviews I have conducted – professionally and for personal interest – with bisexual (across the spectrum), transgender and non-binary (across the spectrum), lesbian, gay, asexual, heterosexual, intersex, poly, kink, cisgender and Queer identified people who span the religious-nonreligious spectrum and were raised all over the world. Since stories – both fictional and non-fictional – are often powerful pedagogical tools for stimulating reflection and discussion about even the most challenging topics, I crafted this novel as a way for readers to see the world experienced by some bi and poly people, and in so doing, hopefully acquire a starting point for discussion and understanding of sexual complexity in contemporary society.

For me, *Homecoming Queens* is a pedagogical text blending my artistic and research endeavors in a manner that has, throughout my career thus far, been incredibly effective in classrooms. In fact, the novel itself developed from my own recognition of the ways such stories could have been useful to people like me growing up in a world where explaining bisexual, poly, and transgender experience – even to fellow Ph.D. holders – remains an exhausting necessity. Further, the novel developed in a social context where many monogamous Americans suggest everyone can now get married legally even though this is not yet true for poly people. As such, *Homecoming Queens* may be used as an educational tool for people seeking to better understand growing numbers of openly bi and poly people; in relation to debates concerning extending marital rights to poly unions; as a supplemental reading for courses dealing with gender, sexualities, relationships, families, religions, narratives, the American south, identities, culture, or intersectionality; or it can, of course, be read entirely for pleasure.

ACKNOWLEDGEMENTS

Thank you to Patricia Leavy, Peter de Liefde, Jolanda Karada, Paul Chambers, Robert van Gameren, Edwin Bakker, and everyone else at Sense Publishers and the *Social Fictions* series for your faith in me, your willingness to support creativity, and your invaluable guidance. I would also like to especially thank Shalen Lowell for your considerable assistance and support. I cannot overstate how much the efforts and support of all you means to me.

Thank you especially to my life partner Xan Nowakowski for giving me the courage to write novels in the first place, and walking by my side as I completed them and sent them out for consideration. My books would not exist without your inspiration, guidance, and faith, and I will never be able to thank you enough for what your support and encouragement means to me.

I would also like to thank Lain Mathers, Kate McCabe, Shay Phillips, and Eric Anthony Grollman for providing constructive comments and insights throughout this process. There is no way for me to express how important your efforts have been to me.

I would also like to thank someone I have never met. This novel was written while I was listening to the works of Brandy Clark nonstop, and her records provided a soundtrack for the writing, editing, and revision of the work.

Finally, this novel would not be possible without the years of research I have done on sexualities, gender, religion, and health. I have had the privilege of interviewing and observing so many wonderful bisexual, transgender, non-binary, lesbian, gay, intersex, poly, kink, asexual, and otherwise Queer people formally and informally over the years, and many of their experiences find voice throughout this novel. I would thus like to thank all of them both for sharing their stories with researchers like me, and for being role models to many of us navigating gender, sexualities and relationships throughout contemporary society.

CHAPTER 1

"Please tell me you're kidding," I say on the phone with Crystal. It's hard for me to keep a straight face at the thought of living in a place called Queens, Georgia with my husband and former homecoming queen wife, but she is serious.

"We need to be here. Daddy's place is too important to the town to just disappear and become a Sonic or something. There is no one else to take it, and I don't want to sell it. I grew up in this building. It's sad enough that it's closed right now. I don't want to think about it being closed forever as long as it can be saved."

"You can't be serious, look, I know I'm a jerk sometimes, but this prank is too far. Do you really expect me to move to the middle of nowhere so some small-town folk can eat the hamburgers they've been eating since the 1960's? This is not funny Crystal." I'm hoping this is another one of her pranks. I'm hoping it's like the time she locked me out of the house when I fell asleep naked on the upstairs front porch at night. I'm hoping it's like the time she set a hidden alarm to go off every night at 2 am after I kept accidentally waking her up. I'm hoping it's like the time she – with Lee's help because she paid him off with designer chocolate – convinced me she had decided she just had to have a kid after all and watched me freak out for two weeks. In many ways, Crystal made a kind of second career of messing with me over the years, but this might be her masterwork. Please, let this be her masterwork.

"I'm not kidding at all, Jackson," oh shit, there is the curse word version of my name, and it hits me that Lee – always the easier one to win an argument with, always the peacemaker in our family – is not on this call. This is an ambush, and I'm outgunned. She really wants me to be the queen that moves to queens with his two loving queens, what the hell is happening to my life. This is all because stupid Chuck had to go and die the night of Lee and Crystal's high school reunion. I want to dig up Chuck and make him pay for this.

"Come on Crys, let's be real here. We have a home in Tampa, we have careers here, we have plans. You want to leave all that behind to take over your dad's restaurant?" Okay, I'm cheating here a little bit. I don't mention that I'll miss all the record stores, that we have Queer clubs we can go to as a trio anytime we want, or the wonderful selection of local breweries. I look at my little can of Florida Cracker, and think about being stranded in Bud Light country with no way out. I want to punch whoever said love is about compromise.

"The house is paid for," she's right. "I can take a leave from school, I have a sabbatical coming up anyway, so I can see how it goes for a year," I hate how smart she is. "You can write from anywhere sweetheart," damn it, I feel like I'm already losing this one. "You can get your records on Amazon, and they actually have a record store here now believe it or not." I should have known she'd see through the practical reasons I offered and get to the heart of the matter, "And Atlanta is not that far away if you want to go dance." Note to self, marry dumb next time. "Lee and I feel like this is something we need to do."

This *is* an ambush, and she took the worst fighter out of the conversation. She's a couple steps ahead of me ready for whatever I say, and I realize that odds are I'm going down. Not without a fight, I think and try to come up with something to shift the conversation. "Where is Lee," I say thinking I can talk him out of this.

"Lee is down at the lawyer's office working on the paperwork with dad's estate so it will be ready for me in the morning, and checking in with the local paper about freelancing," she says almost singing the words because she's knows I don't have a good argument. Okay, this is not going well, time to pull the trump card. It's not fair, but desperate times and all that.

"Have you thought about safety? You have two bisexual husbands who have been – and would like to stay – out of the closet for a long time now. You are also openly bi, and may want to occasionally date other women from time to time like you always have Crystal? Did this factor into your thoughts? What if some redneck decides he doesn't like that very much? Have you thought about that?" I realize I'm being a jerk the moment the words come out of my mouth, but I chalk it up as collateral damage until I hear the pain in her voice.

"You're an asshole Jackson! How dare you suggest I would put my family in danger? And you know damn well I think of the dangers all three of us face every damn day! Of course, I have thought about that – the same way I rushed home at the speed of light hoping y'all didn't go out that night when the bar was lit on fire in Tampa and called you frantically from the conference in Alabama in the middle of the night when the shooting happened in Orlando. The same way y'all freaked out and interrupted Alice and I that night to make sure I was safe after that group of assholes attacked a bunch of the girls leaving the bar over in St. Pete. Of course, I thought about your safety, our safety, and I can't believe you would suggest otherwise." She's right, of course, this was a low blow. Her voice makes it clear she's hurt, and I can't blame her.

I feel bad for a second before imagining myself living in Queens, Georgia. Somehow, the thought of living there removes all the magic and only leaves the terror in Lee's stories. Then, I say, "But you're talking about small town Georgia Crys. I get it, it's dangerous everywhere, but do we even stand a chance in a place like where you grew up? Isn't that a big part of why you and Lee wanted out of there in the first damn place? Have you forgotten how scared you were someone would find out or what it was like when that coach found out about Lee's extra activities when you were both in high school and only his skill on the football field saved him from being outed to the whole damn town? Is this really what you want to go back to now? Do you want to be back in a place where we might be better off hiding?"

"It's not 1998 anymore Jackson! Yes, bad things still happen to our people here and elsewhere WAY TOO MUCH, but there are also good things happening. Augusta started having Pride events a couple years ago, and there are already two people here in the town that are openly out and doing fine here raising their daughter. I know it's not ideal honey, but I think we'll be okay and we can always leave if it doesn't work out. I mean, didn't you say yourself that it was important for more of us to be out and visible in unexpected places."

If it was possible for me to hate Crystal, I probably would have right in this moment. One of the terrible things about loving someone smarter than you is they can often use your own arguments against you after the fact. Why didn't I marry someone I could outsmart? Instead of focusing on Crystal winning this argument with little effort, I just started hating Chuck with all I had. In my head, this was all his damn fault and I wished I could make him pay. I was beaten. I knew it. She knew it. I had no leverage at all. I was done.

I could either stay in Tampa and risk losing the loves of my life who would have every reason to read my absence as a lack of support for them (especially after they'd supported this whole crazy writing dream I had when we got to Tampa years back), or I could get ready to become a queen living in Queens with my queens. In the end, it wasn't much of a decision – they were my family and I did not even want to – even if I could have made myself – imagine my life without them. In some ways, I guess that was how they were feeling about the damn restaurant and town after Chuck's death, but I didn't think of that at the time.

At the time, I wondered if a place in the middle of nowhere had wifi yet. I wondered if there was a bookstore, or something else worth visiting. I remembered a weekend trip we took to Chiefland, Florida, just up the coast from where we lived, and how I barely made it through the trip because I felt so isolated and bored. It was a beautiful town, and as one of the locals pointed out a little too excitedly for my tastes, they had a new fancy Dunkin Donuts coffee shop. The trip had even been my idea because I occasionally stopped there when I was driving around the state fighting against my old friend writer's block. It was a nice place that I hated within two hours. I couldn't wait to get back to the city, and I never wanted even that much exposure to a quiet, peaceful, small town again.

Sometimes we don't get what we want, I thought, and said, "Okay, if you two are sure about this, I'll start looking into what needs to be done down here and when I can get up there."

"Jackson," she said almost immediately starting to sound like the woman who loved me again, "You never know, this could be a lot of fun for you. I know that sounds crazy to you right now, but you do love those Brandy Clark songs and Lee's stories about this place. I mean, hell, remember when you dragged us to hear that Isbell guy and every damn song was a story about small towns in the south? You can experience that world yourself now. Maybe you'll have more fun than you think, and I think you know we'll always appreciate you making this change for us no matter how long we stay. Trust me, I'm sure it's going to work out okay."

There it was, and she knew it. The reason she was winning this one no matter what Lee thought. Even if Lee disagreed as much as I did, we were a team, we supported each other's dreams, and we changed anything and always had to that end. For whatever reason, she needed this – and later I would realize that Lee did too – and in the end, that was enough for me to get on board and at least give it a shot. It was the same way I sometimes needed to go out to Ybor city to meet new guys – especially my favorite tourist – or she sometimes needed someone like Alice to spend nights with or Lee sometimes needed to take random trips to various cities he only knew about from television – we always supported each other's needs.

The fact was, our relationship was built on sharing our needs with each other and trusting each other to always come home, work for the whole, and be open with one another. At various times throughout our marriage, one of us had an urge they needed to follow – me not looking for work and instead trying to write while they supported me when we got to Tampa, for example – and the others had adjusted as necessary to make such pursuits possible. It was this idea that if we trusted each other, we could find a way to make anything work. And there was the point, I did trust her and Lee too, that was the basis for this whole life we had built over the past 12 years. After all, maybe love really was about compromise even at times when you wanted to shoot whoever the hell said that in the first place.

CHAPTER 2

Queens, Georgia was founded as more of an outpost than a town in the late 1800's. There were travelers making their way between Atlanta and Augusta on a regular basis, and a group of farmers decided they could capitalize on this fact. The travelers would pass through the little area and it's farms every few days on their way to and from the markets in the cities and the rivers that carried goods to and from Savannah. They would sit and chat on the benches outside the shops, and buy a piece of fruit or two and a shot of whiskey to pass the afternoon or evening in question. There were rumors that one of the farms owned by an old white family served as a kind of brothel that was very popular.

Like much of Georgia at the time, the place was mostly just farmland with a little patch of shops for the farmers' needs in the middle of the area near a little bit of water – Lake Brandy it was called, which was more like a pond the size of one you might find on a mini golf course than an actual lake and named after the favorite drink of a local farmer described in the history of the town as the ultimate smartass. Unlike much of Georgia at the time from what I could tell by the historical records I was able to access from my home office, the town owed its existence to freed people of color who made up the owners of three-fourths of the farms in the area – benefits of effective reconstruction policies and transformations at the time –until the establishment of Jim Crow in the south led them to abandon the area for other parts of the country where they hoped for a fairer shake   a pattern people of color unfortunately still face in America today. Very few of the townspeople, I later learned, knew this bit of history, but every single one knew about the whorehouse.

By the time Crystal's father Chuck turned 18 in the April of 1964, the days of travelers passing through Queens on their way to and from Atlanta and Augusta were over. The establishment of Interstate 20 in the late 1950's combined with increased use of cars by Americans in general rendered the town pretty well isolated. Augusta remained and expanded about 45 minutes north, and Atlanta existed some two hours by car to the west, but there was no Interstate exit that directly connected these areas to Queens. There still is not I realized with a sinking feeling as I was studying the area hoping to find something good about moving there. Instead, Queens existed outside of the knowledge of most people – even those in nearby cities like Atlanta and Augusta – as a small farming community with a 2 mile stretch of shops downtown. As 1964 passed, and in the rest of the country the rights movements and other activist events shot into high gear, most of Queens was deserted and most of the storefronts – about 12 of them at the time – were empty.

According to the diaries Lee found in the attic the day after Chuck's funeral, which would now live – thanks to the magic of the postal service – in our Tampa home for safe keeping, Chuck considered leaving like so many other young people were doing, but Thelma's mother was experiencing health problems and he had already decided Thelma was the most amazing thing the world had to offer. The two were married not long after his father passed away in an accident at the energy plant 30 minutes away in Waynesboro. Though the details were sealed at the end of the case, Chuck's dad, as the story goes, went to work for the power company after visiting Waynesboro one year for the annual Bird Dog competitions, and enjoyed his work there – including the drive back and forth between the towns – until one night an electrical panel he was working near malfunctioned and sent him to meet Jesus. The power company, to the surprise of many of the workers in the area, accepted responsibility for the accident and paid Chuck a nice sum of money.

On their honeymoon, Thelma told Chuck about a dream she had where their small town became a community bonded together over a shared place or event like Waynesboro with its Bird Dog competitions or the famous bars in Savannah. She wondered aloud about this idea all weekend while they enjoyed the sounds, sights, and little shops on Tybee Island. They kept talking about the idea when they returned to Queens, and they started making lists of the kinds of places or competitions they could start with Chuck's inheritance and feel capable of operating in the town. They chatted with local citizens young and old. They went to the churches and asked for opinions. Uncharacteristically at the time, they even went into the black neighborhoods looking for advice and hoping whatever they built could better unify the town. They spent two years trying to come up with a plan.

On their third wedding anniversary, Chuck and Thelma opened a restaurant in the little downtown area they called "CHUCKS – A QUEENS TRADITION." I found an old newspaper clipping – and many more over the years – celebrating the establishment of the place. It was seen, even at the start, as a new day for the town, and over the years it became a central meeting place. It was in that diner that the citizens – white and black alike according to the photos and comments I found in the newspaper's online archives – met to discuss the race riots that broke out two years later in Augusta. It was in that diner the kids of different races met to await the bus when integration policies finally hit this part of rural Georgia in the 1970's. A candidate for governor had even eaten a burger at the place one day in the 1990's. It had been the first place in the area to host the classic car shows, specialty crafts fairs, and other events that became so common in the deep south in the 1990's and later. It was a hub of activity that reflected the broader changes in the world over the past 50 years.

Fifty years of operation held a lot of milestones. It was in this space that Thelma announced her first pregnancy to a room full of kids celebrating their latest on the field victory in 1970. It was in this space that the first interracial marriage the town remembered or knew about or recognized – maybe all three   held its reception after the vows. It was here that the Bible studies were held when the biggest church in town burned during the lightning storm of 1985, and took six months to rebuild. It was in the same space the other big church did the same after it's building burned due to an electrical issue a couple years later. It was in this place that little Crystal, who was quite adorable from the pictures I found, played wonder woman and other fantasies to the delight of the patrons. It was in this place that little Lee was unfortunately captured on film covered from head to toe in what looked like a wonderful example of the ways kids can break ice cream machines.

It was in this space where the town learned Thelma had, as the paper put it, "the cancer," a few years ago, and where she would meet the group of town's people who supported her as she said goodbye to this planet. It was in this space that Enis Jacobson, the All-Star Basketball player, got his trademark strawberry milkshakes after every game before ever catching broader media attention as the milkshake drinking cross over machine at the University of North Carolina. There was a photo of him holding up a basketball, he was probably in high school at the time a few years before Crystal and Lee would go to that school, wearing a Chuck's shirt and smiling the same big grin immortalized in Sports Illustrated the night he was drafted into the NBA first overall. The more I studied the place, the more it seemed like every major moment in the town in the past half century had something to do with Chuck's.

In many ways, the town itself had grown around Chuck's. After the lean years and youthful desertions of the 1960's and early 1970's, the town began to grow with the influx of new jobs at the power plant over in Waynesboro, and the entrance of corporations like McDonald's and Kmart in the 1980's. McDonald's remained with two locations in town, but Kmart had gone under in the face of the arrival of Walmart in the early 2000's. The building that introduced Queens' residents to big box stores was now a skate park and youth center with only a bit of faded lettering on the far end to suggest it was ever something else. Other corporations arrived, and so did local merchants to meet the modest needs of the families that populated the town. I read about these things, and couldn't stop humming Brandy Clark's "Big Day in a Small Town," and wondering about Methodist men dealing with indiscretions.

As the town grew, there were celebrations and cross-promotions with Chuck's and every week of every year found people gathering there over a burger and fries or a coffee and grits to discuss the goings on. By all accounts, Chuck and Thelma became pillars of the community, and were active in every local organization imaginable. They were there when the bookstore selling used paperbacks opened in 1989. I remember, at first, being very pleased that they at least had a bookstore. They were there when the corner drug store was replaced by a brand-new Walgreens in 2003. They were there when the tire plant opened between the town and another town called Louisville a few years later just before the recession shook the whole country, and they were there as downtown shifted from empty storefronts in the 1960's to small independent shoe stores, repair shops, and clothing stores in the 1980's to a mix of surviving local businesses and empty storefronts in the 1990's to finally a collection of niche goods including a record store – the one Crys mentioned I was sure – and a farmer's mart in the past couple years. I remember thinking I could write an entire Reba McEntire album about Chuck's, and wondering if I would meet Fancy when I got there if the lights stayed on.

From the broad windows of their restaurant, Chuck and Thelma watched all these events unfold, raised their family, and got to know every single person who ever passed through town. They were at the graduation ceremony where Enis promised to make the town proud, and at the trial when little Ralph was tried for killing his daddy after being abused most of his life. They were in the (almost entirely) white church on that fateful Sunday when the traditional worship service was moved to earlier in the morning for the purposes of offering a new service with more modern music later in the morning. They were also there when the White and Black churches started having shared cook outs, and even catered the first of these now annual events. They were there for the weddings, the funerals, the homecoming football games, and the holiday parade every year. They were also there for the unplanned pregnancies, the drunk driving accidents, the biggest deer killed each season, and the introduction of meth and the internet into the community at the beginning of the new millennium.

Looking at photos, it was remarkable both how much the town had changed over time and how little Chuck's place had changed in the same amount of time. It looked older now, and it was obvious it had been painted and renovated a few times over the years, but the old sign still shouted out into the street and the place looked mostly the same. While, according to one of Chuck's journals, the original inclusion of "A Queen's Tradition" was meant to be a joke, flipping through photos decades later it felt a lot more like a prophesy.

CHAPTER 3

"How you doing babe," Lee asks when I answer the phone six weeks after Crystal and I grudgingly agreed our family was moving to Queens. Neither of them have been back home yet, but I have heard from them each on different days. I spent my solitude studying the town, packing and sending things they need for life in Georgia, and storing – and reading some of – Chuck's journals since they arrived at the house three days after I learned I was moving to the middle of nowhere because I fell in love with these country folk.

"I'm okay. I finally got everything set up, and should be leaving in the next day or so to join y'all unless you've hopefully come to your senses?" I know I'm being a whiny brat, but I don't care. My search of the town's history has increased my curiosity, but has not changed my opinion that this is a silly idea at best. I spent each of the days over the last six weeks hoping against hope that they will get sick of the place before I join them.

No such luck, I think as Lee says, "Awe man, come on, it's going to be great! We're having a lot of fun running the restaurant. It's like we're kids again, and Crys has even started looking into maybe doing an oral history project about the town." Great, just what I need, Crys to find another reason to stay in small town nowhere. At the same time, I smile because I was kind of worried she was going to drop her research and end up regretting it in the future. I'm kind of glad she's found a way to do both even if it does increase my chances of living in a small town for more than a little while.

"What about you, and your writing?"

"You know, and I want to talk to you about this, but I think I might write a book. It's very peaceful here, and thanks to Crys' book sales, your book sales, and our family inheritances and savings, we don't really need much income at all from me. I was thinking I might finally try to write the book." Lee had been talking about writing a book the whole time I knew him. He wanted to write about his experiences with sports writing and culture. He wanted to tell his own story, but blend it with things he noticed during his career. Crys and I thought it would be a great book, and once again I found myself accidentally happy about something that might more permanently take me away from the comfort of city life.

"I think it would be a good idea Lee, and you know Crys and I would help you any way we could."

"I'm thinking about it a lot, but we'll see," and that was always what he said whenever this topic came up. "For now, I like managing the restaurant with Crys and I might do some freelance writing for the paper here, and maybe even the Chronicle or the Metro Spirit up in Augusta. Who knows, it's an adventure, and maybe I'll just write a blog about sports or about our move up here or about religion or something like that." This was the Lee I knew and loved – a thousand ideas always coming through his pores, but very few of them ever actually happening. I was always amazed by the distinction between his unending list of plans and my relative difficulty coming up with one idea in the first place. "Anyhow, I just wanted to check in with you, and see what you were up to today."

"You mean you wanted to make sure I was okay now that everything in Tampa is basically finished?"

"Basically," he says with a chuckle.

"I'm okay. I'm just going to sit on our porch, wait for Marcus to arrive, listen to records, and say goodbye to the place." Marcus was our neighbor, and maybe the only person who liked sports half as much as Lee. Marcus was from the south side of Chicago, and moved to Tampa to take a nice job at a bank downtown. Marcus loved this city, and thought it was insane that we were moving to a small town in Georgia. Marcus was going to keep an eye on, and if he wanted to, use our place while we were, as he put it, "hiding in the woods."

"You make it sound like the end of the world Jackson."

"I'm moving to a place called Queens where the biggest building in the area is a Walmart."

Laughing, Lee says, "I know babe, I'm sure we both owe you big time for this one."

Matching his laughter, "You damn right y'all do."

14

"Okay, I love you Jackson, and keep us posted on your trip."

"Will do babe, love you too," I said as we hung up, and I turned the volume back up on my stereo. Michael Jackson's voice came from the speakers, and I started looking over the hard copy I printed out of my latest book again. Editing always calmed me in ways I could not put into words, and I really needed that.

I tried to focus on the novel, but instead, I kept thinking about the first time I saw this house. Crystal had just taken her job at USF, and we were visiting to sign the lease on the townhome we expected to rent. For fun, we went driving through the city, and found ourselves in this neighborhood just off the bay. Crystal stopped the car, and pointed. In front of us, we saw this place standing captured by the sun. It had a porch on both the first and second levels that went all the way across the house. It had what looked like a massive, open downstairs space, and what looked like a small house for a second floor. It was Lee who spotted the writing on the for-sale sign that mentioned a third-floor loft separated from the rest of the house.

Two weeks later, we came back and began aggressively pursuing it. We looked up all the information on the place, learned that it was being sold in a hurry because of family issues, and decided this would be our home. It was only a few blocks from a series of shops dotting the intersection of Bay to Bay Boulevard and MacDill, and it was just far enough from the main roads to be quiet yet an easy walk to the fun shops. We fell in love with the loft, and were certain it was the perfect master bedroom for the three of us. It also had three other bedrooms – one for each of us to make our own space – and a fourth guest room. The kitchen was so big and so well equipped that Lee squealed when he saw it, and Crys and I imagined the dinner parties he was planning in his head that certainly included far too ornate wine lists. One of the smaller bedrooms, on the back of the house on the second floor, had a big bay window that you could sit in, and Crys sat there as we looked through the house the same way she had in our place in Miami while she wrote her dissertation. I was giggling at their excitement until we stepped out onto the house length front porch and images of me writing in this space flooded my brain. I too became a kid in a candy store.

We pooled our resources and bought the house, but we put it in my name for tax purposes – read tax breaks – because we already agreed that Lee and Crystal would be the ones to get legally married – read tax breaks – and there was no way for all three of us to do so. The house would be my link to them legally, alongside many other contracts our lawyer helped us put together to protect our union in a country that did not yet grant equal access to two aspects of our marriage. We sat on the hard wood floors on the first night laughing that our townhouse had already become useless, sipping wine, and fantasizing about the different ways we could decorate the place. As I replaced Michael Jackson's *Thriller* with *Some Girls* by the Rolling Stones, I thought about that night and all the memories made in this place, and more than ever, I did not want to go to Georgia.

A couple hours later, I switched out my coffee for a can of Florida Cracker. I was listening to an old Marvin Gaye album, and looking over the map to make sure I knew where I was going when I left the next day or the day after that. I was having trouble deciding because I really didn't want to leave, but everything here was already done. As I pondered the maps and found a bookstore listed in Milledgeville, Georgia that looked like an interesting stop along the way, Marcus came walking up to the porch with his son Dante. "I'm surprised you're not playing some sad ass country music to get ready for your trip to the woods," Marcus said with a chuckle as Dante started his usual practice of rummaging through my records.

"Nice one, you got anymore because I don't think this is hard enough yet?"

Laughing and slapping me on the knee before taking a seat, he says, "Nah, I feel for you man, I do. I would say I'll visit, but I think they still got issues with people like me up yonder." "Yonder" was drawn out in an attempted Southern drawl I appreciated.

"I'm not sure they'll like me any more than you."

"You ain't wrong there Jacks," he says laughing harder, and continues, "But they can see my black ass coming a mile away while you can just play with your husband and your Streisand records in private and maybe they'll never notice."

We are both laughing harder than I have in a while as Dante comes up to me holding a Natalie Cole 12-inch single from the box. "You want this one little guy," I ask, and he nods in that shy way he always does, and I say, "Go get it DJ," and his face lights up as he changes the records out like a pro. This is just one of the many rituals I know I'll miss more when I finally do leave town the next day or the day after that or sometime next week maybe.

"If it makes you feel any better, your departure is annoying the shit out of Deidre and me," he says cracking open the beer I hand him from the cooler. Deidre is his wife and Dante's mom, and to put it simply, maybe the only person on the planet who makes Crys feel intellectually deficient. She graduated from Florida A&M with perfect marks, three national fellowships, and a powerful position as an engineer down here in the bay. Thanks to her, I know far more about the way this planet works than I ever thought possible even though I'm not sure if I really understand even ten percent of what she's tried to teach me.

"How is my horror annoying you?"

"I told you from day one it was a bad idea to encourage Dante's obsession with records, but no, you just had to infect him with your hipster shit and now that you're leaving, guess what I have to do? Yep, I gotta start going to those dirty ass record stores you take him to, and figure out how to use last century's technology all over again." He bursts out laughing, I'm kind of surprised he kept a straight face through that crap. This is one of our running jokes. He was worried about Dante – they both were – years ago because the kid didn't like anything. Sports, nope. Books, nope. Church, nope. Their jobs, nope. The kid was, it seemed, naturally apathetic to everything. And then, one day, he came over while Marcus and I had beers and made fun of each other, and fell in love. The kid has been obsessed ever since. He will make good grades, for a record. He will go to church and behave, for a record. Hell, the kid will do anything for a record it seems – I even got him to cut the grass for both our houses a couple weeks ago for a box of old forty-fives.

"Well, I could just take him with me, I mean, I could use the company," and at this, we both start laughing harder than is probably healthy. Marcus knows better than anyone other than my spouses that I find the idea of having children equivalent to the idea of being tortured for the rest of my life. I honestly cannot stand most of them, and often wish they didn't exist. There are exceptions, like Dante, that I get along with at least partially because I can take them back like a good movie rented from a store at any time, but overall, I could do without them and have made sure they barely exist in my life. It would take something major I can't imagine for me to ever bring some kid home to live with us.

Laughter and beer rituals accomplished, we leave Dante with the record player, and go inside. I show Marcus where everything is in terms of documentation, storage, and anything else he might need. He already knows the codes to the internet and security system and other technological aspects of the house because he sometimes has parties here with and without Lee when Crys or I are elsewhere, and because sometimes when Deidre is working on an especially stressful project that none of us can understand no matter how hard she tries to explain it, he stays in our guest room with Dante to give her space to think and work without having to worry about the two of them. After about 45 minutes roaming through the house, we find our way back to the porch where Dante is spinning an old Whitney Houston record.

"Come on kid, we gotta get you to music practice." Dante is now learning piano and guitar. As they start to go, I motion for him to come over to me, and he does. I hand him a box I got from one of the local record stores, and inside it, I have put a collection of records he seems to play the most when he is at the house. He grabs it, tears run down his little face, and he hugs the box he has to strain to lift. Marcus smiles at me, I promise to call, and they disappear from my daily life in a way that aches more than I expected. Marcus is the first neighbor I have ever had who I truly enjoyed knowing, and I wonder how rare that might be. I can't help but wonder what the odds of finding another friend like him are when I head for Queens the next day, the day after that, in a couple weeks, or maybe by the end of the year.

CHAPTER 4

The next morning, I ship my necessities to Queens, and pack up the car. Part of me wants to find reasons to stay, but another part of me wants to see my spouses again soon. The neighborhood is quiet as all the families have made their ways to children's schools and parent's jobs. I'm standing in the driveway staring at the other houses, savoring the scene, wondering when I'll see it again, when Alice pulls up in front of the house with Helloween's first album blaring through the sunroof of her blue Honda, and reminding me of metal shows her and Crys took me to at the Orpheum in Ybor City.

Hopping out of her car with her usual never-ending supply of energy, Alice says, "Hey Jacks, you ready to become a redneck," and smiles at me as she moves up the driveway.

"Yep," I say faking a deep Southern drawl like Marcus did though not nearly as well as he did, "Gonna find me a good fishing hole and do it to it." I don't know if this is an actual Southern phrase, but I think I heard it on one of those redneck comedy specials.

Chuckling, she says, "I brought some of Crys' clothes that she wants up there." Alice and Crys have been dating for a couple years now. Almost perfectly proportional in shape, Alice always wears these sun hats over her curly blonde hair, and just seems to have a spark that most people I've met lack. Every day is a holiday in Alice's world. Crys met her one night when she went over to St. Pete to a lesbian poetry night at a side the road bar nestled in a working-class neighborhood. Alice took the stage, and recited a poem she had written about a crush she had on her boss that was intertwined with random lyrics from Alice Cooper's *From the Inside*. The combination of Alice's voice, perfectly proportional body, and utilization of one of Crys' favorite albums created an instant desire. Crys went outside, and as is our family rule, texted Lee and I – we were watching some basketball game or something like that Lee and Marcus wanted to see for some damn reason, I seem to remember hot guys in shorts – that we might need a "conference" soon.

Within our relationship, "conference" was the code word for occasions where one of us found someone new we might want to date, sleep with, or otherwise pursue. We established this code and the rules for it when we first became a serious, committed union because while Lee was more on the monogamous side of the spectrum and would probably have been fine with one partner if he hadn't simply fallen in love with two who were compatible with each other and wouldn't make him choose, Crys and I were a little more complicated. Both of us desired long term, committed, loving relationships, but we also wanted the freedom to pursue other people. For us, the perfect scenario was the three of us as a family, and the freedom to go out and play. We agreed this would be the system, but that all extra-family endeavors would need to be discussed and agreed upon before they became sexual.

While there had been others along the way, Alice was without doubt the most serious relationship Crys ever formed outside of our union. They hit it off immediately, and Crys – for the first and only time in our relationship – found our agreement difficult that first night. There was almost no conversation about it when she got home because Lee and I could both tell right away she found something special. Her whole face and body lit up the same way they were in our happiest moments, and she was blushing with every detail about Alice she shared. By the end of the first morning after Alice spent the night with Crys, Lee and I felt the same way. She was amazing, intelligent, funny, and beautiful, and watching her and Crys interact around the kitchen table while we all had breakfast Lee and I both thought we might be adding a fourth full timer to our family at some point. There was just something about the way they connected that felt right to all of us from the start, and standing in the driveway that day, I thought it was fitting they sent Alice to check up on me.

"You can tell Crys I'm fine, she'll believe you. I'm actually getting ready to leave, and we both know you could have shipped those clothes or visited with them."

Blushing in a way that somehow always made her seem both younger and older than she was, Alice said, "That obvious, huh? I told her you would know what was going on. You know how she is, she just worries about you, hell about all of us, so much." She smoothed her Iron Maiden t-shirt and smiled at the ground.

"I know, she's a sweetheart. She probably also wonders if I'm really going to come up there," we both share a laugh at this, "But how are you doing?" Lee and I were wrong about Alice becoming the fourth in our little family, but not for a lack of interest on Alice's part, or best we could tell, a lack of desire on Crys' part. For some reason, Crys just kept her at arm's length a lot of the time. It was obvious Crys was in love with her, and we made it very clear we loved her too even though not sexually-speaking, which wasn't relevant anyhow in this case, but Crys just avoided any kind of discussion on the matter. According to Lee, Crys had been this way with other women over the years. Crys wouldn't talk about it, but for some reason, there was something different for her about commitment when it came to women. As a result, Alice became part of the family in practice, but not in name and their relationship remained casual even though Crys often got upset by this arrangement. It was like she wanted a commitment – like she had with Lee and I – with Alice, but couldn't do it for some reason that as far as I knew she never shared with any of us.

"I'm doing okay, you know, considering everything, I'm alright," she said looking down at the ground again. "She needs this, I can tell that from talking to her about it, and I get that, but I don't like it. Like you, my first reaction was not, shall we say, kind."

We both laugh for a couple seconds, and I say, "You know she loves you and we do too."

"I know, and I think that's what makes it so hard. I've kind of put other things on hold thinking Crys would come around at some point, but now, with her leaving, I have a lot of thinking to do. She didn't ask me to come, and when I hinted at it, she got upset and the conversation ended so I don't know what will happen there."

"Well, just so you know, you can reach out to me anytime," and I meant that. Alice was one of the most interesting people I knew, and I felt for her deeply. Crys could be difficult in so many ways, but I didn't want to think about how I would feel if she just shut down on me like she often did with Alice when things looked like they were getting serious, and I really didn't know what I would do if she just moved away without wanting me to come. I hoped we would see Alice more, but I remembered Abigail in Miami and how she basically disappeared after we moved to Tampa as Crys just stopped calling her. I also remembered when Crys stopped going with me or Lee to Ybor for a year after things with Jasmine, a youth education researcher from up north, got too serious before Alice arrived in our lives. I hoped we would see Alice again, but past experience taught me that it was unlikely unless this place dramatically changed Crys.

Smiling, Alice says, "Yeah, I appreciate it, but I don't know. Crys seems different since the move, and I think I need to focus on my own life down here," she touches my shoulder and I'm nodding as she says, "Plus, talking to you might not be the easiest thing when I'm trying to figure out my feelings for Crys or life without her."

Continuing to nod, I say, "I know what you mean."

"So, you're heading out today?"

"Yep, I still don't want to, but my family is there so it's not really much of a decision in the end. I want to be angry with them, but like you said, I think they need this."

"Well, you know how Lee gets trips all over the place and new kitchen toys whenever he feels a little down about you and Crys going out with other people?"

"Yeah, what about it?" This was another part of our relationship. Since we wanted everything equal in our union even though Lee rarely – only twice so far – got interested in seeing anyone other than the two of us, we established a system wherein anytime Lee felt like he needed something new just for him, he would get it the same we got new people when we felt the urge. The result was Lee seeing all kinds of places he wanted to on free trips, and having what I can only describe as every chef's dream kitchen. It also meant that Lee could throw as many dinner parties as he wanted, and despite our extreme desire to avoid them, Crys and I would show up at these parties. It also meant there were always far too many sports things – matches, games, I'm not sure – on the television.

"Well, think about what you might be able to get for this one if you hate it there." She giggles and pats me on the back, but the fact is, I have been thinking about how that might work and I was sure they were too. Atlanta was about two hours from the town, a far cry from a fifteen-minute drive over to Ybor, and I had a feeling I was never going to pay for trips to that city. I also had an image in my head of an ever-increasing record collection filling up a whole room of Chuck's old house. Maybe I'd even open my own store at some point. I wasn't sure what it would be, but I was sure I would need some compensation for this particular compromise.

"Honestly, I've been thinking about that. It doesn't help as much as I hoped it would though so I may have to see if Lee can teach me how to be so damn happy about compromises," I say and she lets out a loud laugh. We stand there staring at the street for a few minutes, and she begins helping as I resume the final steps before I leave the house.

A few minutes later, as we are loading the last of my bags into the car, she says, "Well if you want one last party, your favorite is in town again." She smiles at me because we both know who she's talking about. He shows up once or twice every year, and I've been enjoying his vacations for almost a decade now. Generally, he will show up early in the week, stay in one of the hotels downtown, and then I will get a text when the weekend draws near and spend the next week or three on vacation with him. With the weekend only a couple days away, the thought is tempting, but I need to get on the road and I miss my family. Plus, if I put this off, it will likely just get harder next time I try to hit the road. "I saw him at the Kahwa by my building this morning," she finishes and I think about how much he likes that place with its little shiny silver tables and yellow cups.

"I would enjoy that, but I think I'll have to pass this time. Maybe that is the first step in my new life," I say with a chuckle, and she gives me a hug.

CHAPTER 5

While I was studying Queens, I looked over various maps to figure out how to get there. In the end, I decided upon a simple route – I-75 north out of Tampa, and just stay on it until Macon, Georgia. After Macon, I would move through small towns on my way to Queens. First, I would head toward Milledgeville where I noticed a bookstore that might make a nice resting spot where I could get together the nerve for the final leg of the trip. From there, it was an hour or so before I would arrive in Queens. According to my research, the trip should take around seven hours not including random stops to rest, stretch my legs, and evacuate my bladder. It looked easy on paper.

As Alice drove away, I stood there thinking about my studies. I learned almost everything that seemed important to me about Queens, but one thing kept bugging me. Nowhere in any of the materials I could find online was there any indication of where the name Queens came from in the first place. For some reason, it seemed like an odd name for a town in Georgia, and I couldn't locate any reason for the name. Best I could tell, it had been called that for as long as any of the documentation existed, but there were no stories I could locate about the name. As I headed for the interstate, I reminded myself again to ask around town.

Miranda Lambert's voice came through my speakers as I found the interstate exit on Howard Avenue, and merged into the traffic headed north. I wondered if anyone else was on their way to a small town in Georgia because they fell in love with people who decided against all reason to move to such a place. Maybe, I thought, but unlikely. As I drove, I thought about "my favorite," as Alice and my spouses called him. For the first time in all the time I'd – for lack of a better word – known him, I wondered where he came from and what he did there. It was too late to find out now.

My favorite was the closest thing I had to an Alice in the time our family had been together. Unlike Crystal – and Lee on the rare occasion he found someone new to play with – I liked to keep my family separate from my escapades. I didn't want to know anything about the men, women, and non-binary people I dated or fooled around with on the side, and I didn't like for them to know much about me. They did not meet my family, and I didn't even want to know if they had any family. I wasn't looking for connection, I had more than I ever hoped for in that regard with Lee and Crystal. In fact, other than a college romance, my current relationship was the only serious, long term one I ever had, and I didn't need another as far as I was concerned. For me, it was more just going out and having some fun dancing and maybe doing other stuff with strangers who would not bother me afterward or get in the way of my life. I rarely even told any of them my actual name – I liked to go by different names and pretend to be different people – and I didn't care if they told me their own. This practice bought the car I was driving by providing the central element of the plot in my first novel.

I giggled at Lee's reaction the first time he read that novel, and his insistence that I should just call the thing "Slut Bucket" – a phrase he'd heard growing up in Georgia – for fun. As I approached Gainesville that day and a Jason Isbell song began to play, I heard Crystal's response in my head, "Don't you dare do that, there is too much slut shaming in America already." Lee laughed, and so had we. We all knew Lee thought of us as a bit slutty since he'd barely been with almost half a dozen lovers at that point – he hit half a dozen the night of my book release party with a guy named Juan we all enjoyed knowing for the next six months – and had always been the more chaste romantic of our family. In the end, I named the book after my first love, the one from college, River, and I felt good about the decision. I had been on the road two hours when I decided to pull off at Lake City – the term city was used loosely here.

From a trip back from Tallahassee after seeing Deidre give a speech a few years back, I remembered there was a Starbucks to the right off this exit. Lake City was mostly just a couple stretches of road with fast food and other chain stores dotting the sides of the road. We stopped here, and found a wonderful Mexican restaurant that had a nighttime buffet. We spent a couple hours building our own tacos, ignoring the glances of the townspeople when we showed affection that went in multiple directions, and drank too much beer. We ended up staying in a hotel a couple blocks away for the night, a dumpy place that Lee was certain was infested by everything that could possibly destroy our health. In the morning, we found the Starbucks, and then walked through the "mall," which was just four hallways with a buffet on one end and a Belk on the other. As I sat in front of the Starbucks, I wondered if this place would seem big after a few years in Queens.

When I got back on the highway, I marveled, as I often did, at the contraption Crystal set up in the car. It was an old phone I didn't need anymore, and she loaded it with my digital music – as much as would fit in the thing – and somehow set it up where it played on endless, random, repeat while I drove. Gary Allan sung to me about airplanes and lost love as I crossed the Georgia-Florida border. I was enjoying my mocha and thinking about Tifton, Georgia, where my research said the next easy to get to Starbucks was located. Queens, my research told me, did not yet have a Starbucks – or even a fancy Dunkin' Donuts – but Chuck's and a local place both sold coffee downtown so I was hoping that would suffice.

My mind kept returning to my favorite as I drove through Georgia. He said his name was Paul Roman all those years ago during our first encounter and that's what I still called him, but all of us were sure this was a fake name. Hell, my name, Marshall, was fake too so if his was it was only fair. He had the look we had all seen – a tourist who regularly comes to a known Queer area in a city for a week or four and spends time in the bars looking over his shoulder as if significant others and neighbors will walk in at any minute. I didn't care what his real name was, and he had just become my favorite over time in family discussions. Whatever life he led somewhere nearby or far away was none of my business. In fact, part of the reason he was so much fun was because I never had to worry about him asking too many questions, wanting to spend more time together, or any of the other things people did when they said hooray to casual and then changed their mind two adventures later.

Ashley Monroe starts singing about what she'd rather have than roses as I pull into the Starbucks in Tifton. With no real stoppages, I had been on the road about four and a half hours, which was only about thirty minutes more than Google expected and likely about how long I was in Lake City. I was making good time, I thought, getting out of the car to get more Starbucks before entering a world where it wasn't just a few blocks away at all times. I thought about all the time I spent on the covered porch of the Starbucks on Bay to Bay Boulevard editing, and wondered if I would ever do that again. I suddenly felt a little bit of what other people have described to me as homesick for the first time in my life. Maybe I finally put down some emotional roots in Tampa without realizing it.

I used the buttons on the car stereo the way Crystal taught me to set the phone that wasn't still a phone but played music anyway to only play music I had labeled as country for this trip. I was hoping the songs would help my mood, and bring me some comfort as I headed for the country with each passing mile. I didn't know if it was working or not, but I did note that, as Crys and Lee both suggested over the years, I did like a whole lot of this music. The screen on the dash of my car said Travis Tritt was singing to me as I pulled out of Starbucks, and headed back to I-75 North. I continued north passing exit signs for Cordele, Unadilla, and Perry, and wondering what life was like in those towns. As I closed in on Macon, I thought about the couple of days a lifetime ago when I rode the other way to start over in Miami after failing completely in Atlanta.

I moved to Atlanta after college because it was a city I had heard of before, and a friend who interned there the summer before our senior year talked about a booming arts community in the place. I was also trying to get over River who finally left me because he said I had too many "intimacy issues." I figured it would be cheaper than New York, and I told myself I was sick of Houston after four years fighting its traffic and conservatism. I realize now that I had no plan when I arrived in Atlanta, and that was probably not the best way to start a career. I remember I saw a sign in a coffee shop, and took a job slinging drinks. I remember there was a guy named Greg who always seemed to be with some kid who also worked at the shop – who was obviously going through some stuff, and Greg always seemed to know where all the cool parties were. I remember renting a little studio because it was cheap enough for me to afford. I remember I lived somewhere off Moreland Avenue, and that there was an amazing woman named Lena with a tattoo of some Chinese symbol that was very protective of Kid – who she always called "silly" – and reminded me of a girlfriend from high school.

The rest of that year is a blur of alcohol, drugs, naked bodies – including Kid at the very end – and terrible writing that culminated in being thrown out of my studio, fired from the coffee shop, and sleeping on Greg's couch. I remember Kid cried after we had sex the only time we did, and that freaked me out. I remember I didn't see them again after that day. I remember Greg nursed me back to sobriety, and recommended I start over somewhere else. I remember thinking I could love Kid despite being freaked out by the crying, and being scared by the thought so much that I jumped at the idea of leaving. I remember Lena giving me the bus fare to Miami, and trying to comfort me about the way Kid reacted when we slept together. I remember I meant to call or write or email or, I don't know, something when I landed in Miami, but I never did. I thought about all this as I reached Macon singing along to Garth Brooks.

From Macon, I got on highway 49 headed toward Milledgeville. I had been on the road seven hours and some change at this point, and I was beginning to feel tired of the road and my own thoughts. When Tim Mcgraw started singing about going home, I decided I would see about a place to stay the night in Milledgeville. I had been keeping Lee and Crystal posted on my trip, and I knew they would agree that safety outweighed speed. I figured I would get a good night's sleep, and then check out the bookstore I read about. It started when a graduate of a liberal arts school in upstate South Carolina moved to the area hoping to capture some of the creativity of Flannery O'Connor. At some point, she decided to use money from her family to buy an old fire station that was being sold after a new one had been built. For whatever reason, she believed it would make a great bookstore, and the years after would prove her right.

It was after dark when I arrived in Milledgeville. I checked into a motel, and spent about an hour on the phone with Crystal and Lee. They were excited that I would be back with them soon, and I was surprisingly excited myself. I still didn't know what to make of small

29

town life, or if I could possibly like it, but the time apart reminded me how important the two of them were to me. After our chat, I pulled out the hard copy of my latest novel I printed before leaving home, and spent a few hours listening to cartoons coming from the television while not quite working on the draft.

While I kept almost doing work, I thought about all the people that cross our paths. I wondered about the people from Atlanta, my favorite from wherever he was from, Alice from Arizona who arrived in Tampa to fall in love with Crystal and our family, Marcus and Deidre finding each other when he tripped over her purse at a bar, and my own spouses from a small town an hour or so from where I was sitting in a town I didn't know existed until I learned I would be moving. I also thought about River, and how my life might have been different if I had followed him when he got that job in San Antonio. I wondered when I would get a text from my favorite. I wondered how my life might have been different if Crystal had not chosen Miami for graduate school. I thought about all the ways our lives intersect with others in one way or another without ever knowing which intersections matter and which ones simply disappear into the passage of time and the people we had been.

CHAPTER 6

The next morning, I grabbed a quick breakfast and a cup of coffee at a local cafe. Milledgeville was tiny to my eyes, but it also had a certain charm to it. People said hello to each other walking from place to place, and there were all types of independent shops. I wondered if this is what Queens looked like. For a few minutes, I roamed around the downtown area taking in the sights. Something about the old buildings felt comforting to me as I made my way to the old fire house that now held books, art, and according to my ears, Ryan Adams' *Heartbreaker* coming from unseen speakers.

In the front of the shop, there was a table of must read books, and I was quite surprised to see my first novel – the trade paperback version of *River* – perched on the table alongside works by Richard Russo, James Baldwin, Alice Sebold, Stephen King, Alice Walker, and J.K. Rowling. I felt rather honored, and more than a little bit full of myself as I stood there for a few minutes. I did okay as an author, but I was by no means a star or all that highly paid. My work was what a friend of mine who worked in publishing referred to as niche, which I was sure was a code for stories about Queer people and relationships. Personally, I was quite proud of this.

I was leafing through the Richard Russo book I planned to reward myself with once I finished editing my latest book when I heard a squeal, and looked up trying to ascertain the source of the noise. Apparently, I was the source, I realized, as a woman who appeared to be about the same age as I was bounced across the room saying, "Oh my god, are you Jackson Garner?" This was not normal. No one ever recognized me in public. I was not that kind of writer. I lived my life – even visiting bookstores, mind you – without notice, and I was quite all right with this reality. This was, best I could remember, the first time a stranger recognized me in a bookstore. I even enjoyed a wonderful moment a few years ago when some lady in Orlando filled my ear with all the reasons people like me were – she was holding and at times shaking my first novel – ruining the world without noticing that I was kind of a match for the picture on the jacket of the book. I didn't know how to respond to this squealing lady with her beautiful auburn hair and gaping grin.

Stuttering and not at all accomplishing the cool, detached demeanor I had whenever I dreamed about this moment, I said, "Uh, yeah, I am, do we know each other, uh, miss?"

Ryan Adams was singing about a fruit stand as she said, "No, you're funny Jackson, can I call you Jackson," I nod and she continues, "I know you from your books. This is such a treat!" She reached out and shook my hand with more force than I would have expected her little body could contain. I remembered the men who got so uncomfortable with Crys' firm handshakes at her work events, and wondered if there was some training program that taught women how to do this. I needed that class. My own handshake was more like a wave, soft as a feather and moist from the anxiety that always crashed into me when I met people while sober. She was grinning, and I figured I should say something. What do you say when a random bookseller in a small town recognizes you as a novelist whose work she sells? I needed a class on that too before or after I learn how to develop a decent handshake. Smiling, she says, "I'm Lisa, and this is my little shop."

"I'm sorry, uh, I'm just not used to being recognized like this. I don't really know what to say, but I'm touched."

Giggling, she says, "Really? I guess I always thought authors were like celebrities or something, hmm, anyway, I'm such a fan."

Smiling and starting to relax, I say, "Well, some of them are celebrities, or some of us I guess, but not me or at least not yet. I'm glad you like the work."

"What are you doing here? Are you researching a book?"

"No, I, no, I actually just finished my next book so I'm more into editing right now."

"Ooh, what's it about? Oh no, I'm sorry, you probably hate it when people ask stuff like that," she said twirling her hair with the fingers of her left hand.

"No, it's fine. This one is about a couple of women who grow up in a small town in Florida before moving to Chicago to build a life together and open an LGBT bookstore. The book follows them as they experience a lot of surprises, wins, and losses along the way, and is set up alongside music they hear coming from the record shop below their apartment. It's kind of like a Nick Hornby type style of writing that elaborates on the ups and downs of starting fresh in a newfound city." It sounded cooler saying it to someone else than it did in my own head, and I remembered Lee always saying I was too hard on myself. I chuckled at the thought.

"Ooh, sounds fun – so is it like a musical romance thing?"

"Kind of, the music store serves as a vehicle for the main characters to get to know the city itself and themselves."

"That's going to be a good one. So, if not for a novel, what are you doing in the middle of Georgia in my bookshop of all places? You don't exactly strike me as the small town type in your novels." It was true. I often made fun of small towns and characters from them in my books. I didn't know why I started doing that, but it had become a pattern in all three novels so far.

"I hope it's a good one," I say smiling and really hoping we are right about it because it's my last novel on this contract and I really want to keep doing this. "As for here, well, my spouses grew up a little over an hour from here, and the three of us are moving there to take over my wife's family's restaurant for reasons I don't really understand."

She walks over to a nook with coffee and pastries as I speak. She pours herself a cup and asks if I want one. I do, and we sit at one of the four tables with our coffee as I finish speaking "So, you're moving to the area," she says, "How do you feel about that?"

"Conflicted honestly. I love my spouses, but I know nothing about small towns except for their stories about them. I'm not sure what to expect."

"I would guess the "spouses" alone might lead to some interesting conversations in these parts," she says with a laugh. "What town are y'all living in?"

"I think your guess is right. It's a little place called Queens."

"Oh, I know Queens! It's a cute town, and you gotta check out Chuck's when you get there, it's like a tradition."

"Well, actually, Chuck's is the restaurant we're taking over."

"Really? Oh my, y'all are going to be celebrities over there. Wait a minute, is one of your spouses Crystal? Are you the husband she's waiting on?"

"How did you know that?"

"Small towns sugar, gossip travels faster than the speed of light. Crystal has already been in here. She came in one day, and I chatted with her for a few minutes about her move and she checked out the selection because she said one of her husbands – I guess you – would need a good book store when he got here and she wasn't impressed by the one in Queens. I did wonder at the time what she meant by "one of," but I guess now I know. Honestly, and this is not me trying to steal your business, just my opinion, but the one over there is not much at all. Also, one of my regulars – the pastor at the big church, the one that is mostly white people, just beyond downtown in Queens – told me about Chuck passing away, and that his daughter would probably be coming in to take over or sell off the restaurant last time he was here. He said she, Crystal of course, grew up there and went to high school with him, but he didn't mention you or the other husband. I guess now I just need to meet your husband to be all caught up."

"Oh great, we've caught the attention of the religious leader in the town? That can't be good, can it?"

Laughing, she says, "In most cases, no it probably would not be good, but David, that's his name, is not your typical small town pastor. He's pretty open-minded, and he does a lot of work with the Black churches in Queens and even occasionally goes to work with the support groups at the gay church in Augusta. Especially for these parts, he's liberal, and more about the 'do unto others' stuff than the hellfire and damnation stuff. He comes in here with his wife a lot. They're good people, I think, and probably not going to give you trouble. His wife grew up here, and is a major romance reader – and I mean the hot and steamy stuff – and both have read your books."

"A preacher and his wife read my books?"

"Don't be close minded Jackson, people are complex. And yeah, they read your books. I think they may have been a little surprising to David at first because when he first picked one up and opened it, he dropped it on the floor and looked shocked. It was hilarious, but I guess you caught his attention because he took the thing home and came back raving about it. Linda, that's the wife's name, also loved it, but she didn't seem to have the same shocked reaction, probably because she is really into sexual, you know hot and even erotic, fiction, which, a friend of hers I know, who has known her since high school, thinks might have something to do with a less than fulfilling bedroom back at home if you catch my drift."

"Maybe preachers and their spouses are a market I should consider for my work," I say and start laughing. Lisa laughs too, and after a sip of coffee, I say, "Well, you seem to know the area a bit," to which she nods, and I continue, "Any other poly people you know of around here?"

"Not that I know of, sorry. There might be some, you know how it is, but no one open enough for me to have heard of it yet."

"That's what I figured."

For a few minutes, we just sit there, and then she goes to change the record to some soft jazz. "Wow, I can't believe I'm having coffee with Jackson Garner, this is so cool."

"I'm glad to be of service," I say with a fake little bow and she giggles. "If you ever want me to, I'd come over here to do signings or readings – it's a nice spot and I may become a regular."

"That would be great!"

"So, are you a local like Crystal and Lee, sorry, that's my husband's name?"

"Lee, okay, I like that. A local? Me, oh hell no," she says laughing. "I grew up in Charlotte in one of the fancy gated communities, and only came here after college because I was obsessed with Flannery O'Connor. My girlfriend in college and really my first real love, her name is Abs, grew up not far from here, over in South Carolina across the river from Augusta, and told me all kinds of stories about this area, and it just sounded so different from Charlotte or at Winthrop while I was in college. So, I decided to take a year off before starting an MFA program, and I came down here thinking I would find some inspiration. Instead, I kind of found a home – for me and my art – and I've been here ever since."

"I think I'm going to replay everything you just said in my head the whole time I'm here hoping for a similar outcome."

"Are y'all planning to stay long term?"

"I don't know. Lee, you know, our husband," and she nods, "Quit his job at the paper in Tampa and Crystal is on sabbatical from the university for the next year so the plan is to try it out. Officially, that is the plan." She nods, and refills her coffee. "Unofficially, I think they both need to be here for some reason, and I think it may be more of a long-term thing. In any case, I'm preparing for the long term just in case I have to face that." As I speak, I wonder if Chuck is laughing at me from somewhere beyond the grave.

"I can understand that, and I guess you can ride out here anytime the town gets too small for you," she says with a smile, and I'm sure I will spend a lot of time doing just that.

CHAPTER 7

I spent most of the day chatting with Lisa, and after she closed the shop, we went and grabbed dinner. I called Crystal and Lee to fill them in and tell them I was going to spend another night in Milledgeville. Crystal was expecting this and asked a few questions about Lisa that gave me the impression she might be interested in getting to know her better. Lee pouted a bit because he made my favorite meal, but finally he admitted that I should enter Queens – a funny phrase in hindsight – in the way that best suited my needs. They were hanging out at the house having just finished setting up a new turntable they picked up in Augusta the week before in preparation for my arrival. We said our goodbyes, and Lisa asked if I wanted to take a walk. We strolled through the same downtown area I walked around earlier in the day laughing about the most terrible books we had ever read.

Trace Adkins' voice came through my speakers as I pulled to a stop at a faded red, white, and blue sign on the side of the road that read "Welcome to Queens" on the outskirts of the town. I stopped by the bookstore for coffee and a muffin with Lisa before heading out in the morning. She was reading a Virginia Woolf novel and listening to Wilco's *A Ghost is Born,* and I noticed that following the previous evening we shifted from handshake to hug greetings. I somehow felt better about heading to Queens now that I knew there was a place nearby I would enjoy spending time at in the future. We chatted about nothing, and after a half hour I hit the road.

I sat there parked by the sign for a few minutes not sure what I might find on the other side. Crystal and Lee couldn't wait to leave this place when they were younger, and Lisa found a life in a place just a little bigger down the road. What awaited me, I wondered, as I switched off the stereo and rolled down my window. I wanted to take it all in. I wanted to feel whatever was there in case I needed to recall it later. I wanted to find a way to like this place just in case it was a long-term need for Crys and Lee. I wanted to stay there for a while, but instead, after a few minutes, I entered the town on the main road.

The main road past the sign was still just country for about four miles, and then I came to a sign advertising "Matt's flea market – Open every Saturdays and Sunday – Bring the Family." I smiled at the little tables and the covered buildings that likely held even more tables, and wondered what the place looked like on the weekend and if the "s" at the end of Saturday was intentional or not. I continued into town, and a few seconds later, I passed the first gas station and the first red light in the city limits. The cross street was called Springs Road, and I would later learn that along with its parallel cousin, Falls Road, about 6 miles straight ahead, it was the unofficial marker of the town to the people who lived there. Within that 6 miles, the main road, aptly named Queens Boulevard, was split into two three-mile stretches with roads on each side leading into neighborhoods and businesses like Mac's Auto Repair, McDonald's, the Super 8 Motel, Tim's Flowers, Lisa's Designs, Burger King, Wally's Sports Bar, Dollar General and Lucille's Balls, which was, for me, a well named sporting goods store.

This stretch of road – from spring to fall or the other way around depending on how one entered the town – looked like so many other small towns I had seen in person or in pictures over the years. The local businesses were situated between the corporate chains, and on the other end of town, almost as if an exact replica, the same gas station sat on the corner of Falls Road followed by a Walmart followed by another welcome sign. Along the way, little streets wove their way back into neighborhoods on each side. The town spread out in that direction for three miles on each side as well, and Lake Brandy sat right in the middle on the left most side parallel to a lumber yard on the right most side. The Walmart, Flea Market, lake, and lumber yard – it was called Mitchell's Got Wood – created a square perimeter around the rest of the town. According to my research, the town had around 2500 people living in it, but aside from Queens Boulevard, the downtown area, and the four points of the square, the rest of the town was only houses and wooded lands. I drove the main stretch all the way to the Walmart that day, and turned around to get a good view of the whole place.

In the middle of Queens Boulevard, there was a set of three parallel streets that ran from the lake at its center to the lumber yard and vice versa. The middle street was called Main Street, and the ones on each side were North Main and South Main respectively. This was downtown. North Main street held an assortment of houses for about four blocks on each side of Queens Boulevard, and then turned into neighborhoods and trailer parks heading out each side. South Main Street was exactly the same from start to finish. I drove both streets fully aware of the moment I first passed our new – Chuck's old – house. It was right on the corner of South Main Street and 3rd Avenue. On each side of Queens Boulevard, the numbered avenues started at 1 and continued until the edges of town.

Chuck's house – our house – was an old bungalow style, two story home with a gaping front porch that looked out toward Main Street. It had been painted a soft green color at some point in history, and had huge bay windows – the kind Crystal loved the whole time I'd known her – along the bottom level, and what looked like standard bedroom windows dotting the second floor. There were two driveways, one on South Main and one on 3rd Avenue, that connected in the backyard. They connected right in front of one of the nicest back porches I had ever seen. There was also a shed, or work building as Lee called it, in the back yard that housed far too many unfinished projects.

After driving the length of both South and North Main Streets, I finally turned around in front of the lumber yard and started driving down Main Street. Main Street looked like any other street in the town aside from Queens Boulevard until I got about four blocks from Queens Boulevard itself. Here, downtown, or what little downtown there was, really began. There was a Walgreens and then a row of storefronts with signs like Jenny's Books, Monique's Salon, Knits n Things, The Vinyl Nest, School Supply, and Sam's donuts leading up to Queens Boulevard. On the other side of the boulevard, the side we were going to be living on, the storefronts continued until I reached the corner of 3rd and Main Street where "Chuck's – A Queens Tradition" stood in its own lot as it had for so many decades. Across the street was an auto repair place – run by someone named Darryl by the name of it – and then the storefronts continued again for another two blocks.

When I got to the end of Main Street, I found myself staring at two churches on each corner across from the "Lake Brandy Recreation Area." The recreation area was simply a handful of picnic tables, and a couple of fire pits with a playground off to the side and a beach leading to the edge of the water behind them. The churches, however, were quite the sight. Both were larger than I expected, and each one was built with ornate details – crevices and stained glass depicting stories and scriptures – and columns that looked like they were built in pre-modern times. The one on the left, the "First Baptist Church of Queens," had a wide expanse of green grass with a walkway leading up to massive wooden doors. The one on the right, the "Queen's AME," had wading pools on each end of a large grassy expanse, and a middle path that led up to dark wooden doors that appeared to swing out on hinges.

In my research, I located another 12 churches in the area, but these were the big ones. Both were once downtown, but moved out by the lake after their original buildings were destroyed in separate events. In the case of the AME, the original building burned down in 1988 due to a wiring mishap that also took out three storefronts located near the church. Apparently, the town's officials missed or ignored a problem with some of the wiring, and one night two blocks went up in flames. In the case of the Baptist church, the lightning storm in 1985 – the same storm many believe caused the later wiring issues – took the original building in its passage through the town. All the records I found said the entire town came together during both events, and each of the churches played major roles in re-building the other when fire decided it was time for a new location.

After staring at the churches for a little while, I headed back to the heart of town. A few minutes later, I found myself parked outside of Chuck's. It looked like something out of a different time, which made sense when I considered that it was. It was a square concrete lot, and along each side there were spaces for cars to park and little speakers for the drivers to order from – though I would learn the speakers no longer worked and hadn't been used in years. In the middle, there was a diner in the shape of a T that began in the back of the lot, and extended most of the way back to Main Street. At its very end, there was a little outdoor seating area as well. Inside, I could see tables set up, people eating and laughing, but less hustle and bustle than I would have expected on a weekday afternoon. I thought about going inside, but decided my debut into small town society could wait.

I turned onto 3rd Avenue, and found myself at Chuck's – our – house on the next block. I pulled into the driveway, pulled around to the back of the house, and saw our other car sitting there taking in the sun. It was quieter than I expected sitting there in the driveway, and I fished my phone out of the pocket of my shorts. I called Lee, no answer. I called Crystal, no answer. I left them both the same message. "I'm at the new house, and I'm staying right here for now." I got out of the car, listened to a couple birds I was sure were laughing at me, and checked underneath the potted plant – exactly like Crystal described it – for my key. Key in hand, I went inside, and quickly learned that no one else was home.

The back door led into the kitchen, which was almost as large as the one in Tampa, and then I found myself in a living room that curved around the house. I stood in one of the bay windows silently admitting it was a nice place. Beyond the living room, there was a den with a pinball machine, an old beat up sofa, and a nice new turntable and stereo system on the wall. This room felt almost made for me, and I wondered if it looked anything like this – framed record covers on the wall, dusty old books stacked on the floor – a couple weeks before I arrived. It did not, Lee told me with a laugh the next day. I left the den, checked out the downstairs bathroom, and headed upstairs. The upstairs had a master bedroom and bathroom combo on one side of the house, and three other nice sized bedrooms that shared a bathroom on the other side. I liked the hard wood floors, and I was glad the place had almost as much space as the Tampa house, but I didn't know what to make of all the pictures of Chuck, Thelma and various town's people scattered all over the walls or the furniture I was sure was bought in the 1970's.

I must have spent more time than I thought in the house because the sun had moved when I came back outside to unload the car. I didn't know where my stuff was supposed to go, or even how they had the place arranged. I had not bothered to ask many questions about their day-to-day life in the town to that point, preferring my own pouting instead. As such, I unloaded the car, and simply put my stuff in the living room in a big pile against the wall under one of the bay windows. I was in the kitchen looking for a drink when I came across a surprise. On the counter over by the toaster, there was a pack of Camel cigarettes. Was Crystal smoking again? When did that happen, I wondered, and then thought, what the hell? I took a Camel and a beer out of the fridge, went out on the back porch, and sat back for a few minutes puffing, sipping, and taking in the scenery of my new backyard.

After three of Crys' smokes and a couple beers, I was feeling pretty relaxed when Lee finally called me back. He was over at Chuck's and Crys was too. It was an unusually busy night he said and I hoped that meant more people than when I passed the place earlier in the day – something about a championship game – and they would be there for a while. They invited me over, but I declined saying I was tired and wanted to relax. We got off the phone, and I wondered about the cigarettes. Crys and I both smoked regularly when we met, and Lee used them occasionally – mostly after sex – but we had mostly given them up five years ago with only a few horrible fights along the way. Except for the occasional shared one on our porch after a really hard day or the occasional couple when out on adventures, we both got rid of them – except for our celebratory packs after submitting each novel or research project respectively, of course – to the delight of Lee. So, I wondered, why was there an almost full pack on the kitchen counter? They were her favorite brand too. I wondered what had led to the shift in behavior, and if I should be concerned about it.

I was too tired to be concerned. I put out the fourth cigarette, polished off the fourth beer, and went inside. The couch in the living room looked especially comfortable to me at that moment. I climbed onto it thinking I would just lie down and rest for a few minutes. I thought about my last couple days, and I wondered what Marcus, Alice, "my favorite," and the rest of Tampa were doing at that moment. I thought it might be fun checking out the town the next day, and I wondered what the coffee at Chuck's was like. I was just resting for a few minutes, I told myself, but apparently, I didn't listen.

CHAPTER 8

I woke up to the sound of eggs cooking in the kitchen. Lee was humming one of those Maroon Five songs he liked so much, and my favorite blanket was wrapped around me. For a minute there, I thought I was in Tampa and that it had all been a weird dream. I chuckled to myself at the absurdity of us moving to a small town in Georgia, but then I realized this was not the couch in the Tampa living room. I opened my eyes and saw a picture of Chuck on the wall. It was no dream. I was waking up on my first day as a resident of Queens, Georgia.

"Sounds like you're coming back to life sleepy head," Lee says with a giggle before sliding onto the edge of the couch and tickling me.

"Okay, okay, I'm up," I say laughing, and he holds me close to him for a few seconds until I say, "Yeah, I missed you too."

"You were out cold when we got home," he says loosening his grip on me. "We were exhausted ourselves from the wave of people coming in celebrating the kid's championship. It was insane babe, just wild. It was especially nice since business hasn't been so good since we took over the place. Anyhow, you were so cute here on the couch, so we figured we should all just get some sleep."

"Yeah," I say smiling, "Sorry I didn't feel like meeting the town yet."

Laughing, he says, "Are you kidding? I'm just amazed you're actually here."

"Oh ye of little faith," I say with a chuckle and pull his head down to my chest. "You know I'm lost without you two bumpkins."

"Ha! That might be true come to think of it, I mean, you haven't learned to cook or manage money so far so I guess at the very least our adult skills come in handy."

"And I happen to love you a little bit."

"But just a little bit right, don't get clingy," he says laughing and getting up from the couch. "Come on, get your cute little butt some breakfast."

Shaking out the cobwebs, I stand up and follow him to the bar that serves as a barrier for the kitchen. He hands me a cup of coffee and a plate of grits and eggs – damn this man knows what I love, I think smiling. "What," he asks.

"Nothing, just glad to be doing this again."

"Even in Queens?"

"The jury is still out on Queens, but yeah, even in Queens it's good to see you again."

"Better than Lisa?"

"Really Lee? Really? You do know I don't fuck everyone I meet, right?"

Laughing, he says, "I didn't get that memo."

Chuckling, I say, "Where's Crys?"

"She's still sleeping. She went to bed after I did last night. She's been up later most nights either out walking around town or sitting on the back porch."

"Smoking?"

"Yep, I saw you borrowed some as y'all used to say."

"Should I be worried?"

"I thought you'd be happy since if she is again I can't really give you a hard time, now can I?"

"I don't mean the smoking, I don't care about that. What is causing it?"

"Crystal has some memories here, and not all of them are good. But, I don't know, I wouldn't be worried. She's Crys – she can handle pretty much anything, you know, and I'm sure she'll be fine."

"What's eating her?"

"She'll have to tell you in her own time babe."

"Oh, come on, not even a hint?"

"You know how it works, we all have our own things and this is her stuff. Not my place to tell you about it just like we knew if you came here it would have to be on your own time so I didn't push you too much and neither did she."

"Okay," I say thoroughly enjoying the grits, "But you're sure I shouldn't be worried?"

"Yeah, I think it's okay and I'll let you know if I feel otherwise."

"Okay," I say watching him wash a dish and staring at the little scar on his forearm that has always mesmerized me. "So y'all are running a restaurant?"

"Well, kind of. Crys is running the books, doing the orders, and handling the financial stuff. You know, the stuff that confuses the likes of you and me," I nod and he continues, "But I'm running the operation of the place day-to-day, and having a good time. You know how much I love cooking," I nod sliding more eggs into my mouth, and thinking about how much we all love how much Lee loves cooking, "It's basically that, just a lot of fun making food for people, hearing their stories like when I was a kid, and that kind of stuff. I don't know, I really like it a lot so far and the regulars are really great, really supportive."

"What about the other folks in the town?"

"It's hard to tell. We're the big gossip, ever since we told them about you, and the reaction has been mixed, business is down a little bit at the restaurant, but I'm sure it's no big deal and will be fine. What matters is we're having a good time, and we're happy to have you back where you belong."

"You better be talking about with y'all and not here in Queens."

"Oh, come on, can't we just enjoy the good stuff for a little bit?"

"Okay, okay, I'm glad you're having fun at Chuck's. It sounds great, I'm happy for you," I say, and I actually mean it. Lee is swimming in a grin, and just seems more alive than I have seen him in years. This might be a good place for us if the effect is half as positive on Crys. I finish my breakfast, and take a sip of my coffee, "Thank you as always for the lovely meal," I say as I get up to wash the dish.

"My pleasure babe," he says patting me on the butt as I move to the sink. "So, what is the deal with Lisa at the bookstore?"

"I like her," I say and his eyes begin to widen, "I don't know if I like her like that so stop with the eyes," he laughs at this and I continue, "But Crys might like her that way."

"Really? Did she say something?"

"Nope, but she had a lot of questions about Lisa."

"Nice, good for her, or you, or both I guess," he says giggling.

As if summoned by the conversation, Crys comes around the corner from the stairs up to the second floor, and enters the kitchen loaded with hugs and kisses for both of us. She holds me tight – much like Lee did – for a few moments, and whispers, "Thank you."

"Was there ever any doubt," I whisper back, and she somehow pulls me in even tighter. Sometimes I swear this lady does steroids when we're not looking because otherwise I just don't know how such a tiny body can be so damn powerful. I remember one time, early on in our lives together, I tried to challenge her in arm wrestling. I don't think my arm has ever properly healed if I'm being completely honest.

"You want any breakfast babe," Lee asks, and Crys shakes her head no, grabs a cup of coffee, and heads out on the back porch for a smoke. Lee and I share a look, he sighs, and then he nods in the direction of the back porch. I kiss him on the cheek, and head for the porch.

When I come outside, Crys is lighting a smoke, "Don't say anything negative or I'll pull the dead daddy trump card on you," she says with a smile.

"You going to share," I say, and she hands her lighted one to me, and lights another one. We sit there in silence for a few minutes as we have for years. "How are you doing Crys? I mean, for real, how are you doing?"

"I'm okay," she says her voice softening a bit. "There are a lot of ghosts in this town Jackson, and not all of them are of the Casper variety. It's been an adjustment with dad dying and talking to people around here. I'm okay, but I'm also tired, sad, and still adjusting. Does that make any sense?"

It made perfect sense to me. I was feeling all the same things, but for different reasons. "Yep, it sounds like what I would expect in this situation, but I had to check."

"And I love you for it."

"You'd do the same."

"Did you know I used to do my homework on this porch?"

"I did not."

"I loved this spot when I was little. I would sit here for hours with my diary and dad would write in his journals. It was nice. Then, when I got older, I would sit out here doing my homework and listening to the birds and watching the squirrels play. Something about this spot is just me, I guess, I don't know how to put it into words. Did you have anything like that growing up? Some place that just felt like it was you through and through?"

"Nope, can't say that I did. It sounds kind of beautiful to me, but I think the first time I had something like that was at our place in Tampa. I think that was why it was harder to leave than I would have expected – like, maybe I had finally put down some roots. I'm not saying it's the same thing, but somehow that helps me understand what you're talking about."

"We had a good life down there, didn't we?"

"Yes, we did."

"We could be back there very soon, or maybe we'll be here for a while. I'm not sure yet, but I'm glad you're here either way."

"Nowhere I would rather be," and in that moment, it was true. I was home – even if it didn't feel like home yet – with my spouses, my family, my roots. If there was a core of me, like this back porch for her, maybe that was it. "We'll stay as long as y'all want."

"So, then what are you going to do with your time?"

"First, I'm going to explore every inch of this place, and hopefully gain like ten or twelve more people who have as many stories as Lee does."

"There won't be any shortage of stories. With nothing else around, stories and gossip kind of run small towns like this one."

"Now that part of Queens sounds fun."

Laughing, she says, "And after that?"

"After that, I honestly don't know. I have to finish editing this book, and I hope they want me to write another one or forty, but I really don't know. I think I'll just see what happens, and like you, I'll probably just need to adjust."

As I finished speaking, Lee stepped out on the back porch. "I'm going to go get the day started. What are y'all up to?"

"I'm going to unpack as soon as one of you tells me where to put my stuff," I say.

"I'm going over to Augusta to talk to the suppliers, we have to order less until business picks back up," Crys says.

"We don't really have any organizational plan yet, we were waiting on you, so I guess pick a room and unpack as you wish. We did turn the den into a Jackson room for you, and we can all share the master bedroom here like we did before in Tampa. So, pick whichever of the other rooms you want, and we'll take the other ones I guess. Sound good?"

Crys says, "Yeah, that sounds good to me."

Nodding, I say, "Well, then I'm going to unpack, and then I'll probably come over to the shop to see you at work hot stuff."

Smiling, Lee says, "And I'm guessing that's the closest you'll get to working in the restaurant, right?"

"Nope."

"NOPE," they both say a bit loud and obviously surprised.

"Yep, I might edit some pages in a booth at some point," I say chuckling at them for even thinking for a second I might have decided to work in the restaurant. We all know I can't stand anything that even sounds like it might involve manual labor or getting dirty.

"That's more like it," Crys says lighting her second smoke of the day. "It's so good to have you both here and together again." Lee and I both nod, each place a hand on her shoulder, and she smiles at us.

CHAPTER 9

After I got situated in the house, I decided to check out Chuck's. There was no one sitting outside when I walked up, and so I went inside with a mixture of curiosity and trepidation. On the one hand, I heard so much about this place and these people that I honestly could not wait to experience it for myself. On the other hand, I was in small town Georgia, bisexual, and in a poly marriage so I wasn't sure what to expect. Could we kiss hello here or should I play it straight when I entered? Could I talk about our life together or was that more of a private thing in these parts? A thousand other questions ran through my head as I pushed open the glass door to the dining room, held my breath just a little bit, and hoped for the best.

When you entered Chuck's from the door on either side of the dining room, you were greeted by the sight of a long bar that stretched across the top of the T shape formed by the restaurant. I came in from the left, and as I walked in, I saw the pathway to two gender neutral restrooms – they just said restroom on them and looked like single occupancy spaces based on the size – on the left side of the bar, and another pathway that I knew went to a storeroom and office on the right side of the bar. Beside me as I came in sat a jukebox that looked like the kind I'd seen in diners all over the country. It was playing an old Drive-by Truckers song. The bottom part of the T began next, and extended with tables on each side of the glass walls all the way to the end where a gigantic set of two booths closed off the restaurant's seating area.

I intentionally missed the lunch rush – if there was one these days – and came in well before any potential dinner rush. There were no people in the bottom of the T, but there were a handful of people sitting at the bar. I was hoping they were the supportive regulars. Behind the bar, a flat top grill and an assortment of cooking and drink materials lined the wall with a room off to the left – parallel to the bathrooms – that I knew housed the rest of the kitchen. Lee was behind the grill working on what looked like a plate of eggs with cheese and sausage in them. His back was to the door so he didn't see me come in, but a couple of the people sitting at the bar turned to look, nodded, and went back to their business.

I kept thinking Lee needed one of those paper hats the grill operators in some old television shows wore when they stood behind similar looking counters. I also found myself imagining younger Lee who had this same position at times during high school. I remembered how fondly he spoke about those times over the years, and how excited he seemed to go to work this morning. A waitress without a uniform – the pad was the only indication she worked there – emerged from the back room to the left, and motioned for me to sit anywhere. I smiled, and took a seat at the bar a couple stools away from the nearest patron. She came up and asked what she could get me, whipping out a pen she had hidden in her red hair.

"I would really like a date with the cook," I said, "But I'll settle for a good cup of coffee."

At the sound of my voice, Lee turned around, and said, "Hey babe" before coming over and giving me a light peck on the cheek. So, I thought, maybe a little affection is okay here.

The other people at the bar were laughing and the waitress screamed, "Oh my gosh, you're Jackson aren't you?"

To this, an older man I would later learn went by the name Richard and practically lived at the place, said, "He better be or our boy Lee might be in some serious trouble," which led to chuckles around the room.

The waitress came bouncing out from behind the bar, and wrapped me in a tight hug before I knew it was happening. Crushed in her vice grip, did every woman I meet lift weights professionally or was I just this weak myself I wondered, I watched the others at the bar first chuckle, and then kind of form a circle around me. As her grip let up and I finally started to feel my hands and feet again, she said, "I'll get you some coffee honey," and bounced back behind the counter – damn she was quick.

Richard introduced himself, and then said, "So, Jackson, be a good fella and explain to me this whole trio thing? How does that work? Tight lips over there won't say nothing."

Chuckling, I say, "Well our Lee is a little shy," as my surprisingly tasty coffee arrives. I'm honestly surprised this is the first thing out of the gate, but I would learn that everyone in town had been trying to figure it out since Lee and Crystal first mentioned me a few weeks ago. They correctly guessed that I would have the most fun with this. "I guess it's about the same as any other relationship. We all fell in love with each other, we had a ceremony when we decided to spend our lives together, and we support each other like other married folks do. For the most part, it's about the same as monogamy from what I've seen, but just with more people and more options in our case."

"So, uh, do y'all, you know," Richard sips his coffee and it's kind of adorable to watch his discomfort. The other people – all male except for one I later learn is named Doris who also practically lives here – stare with obvious anticipation. Maybe gossip really does trump everything else in small towns. Richard continues, "Hmm, do y'all all sleep together, like in the same bed and stuff?"

Smiling, I say, "Sometimes we do, sometimes we each sleep in separate beds. Sometimes Lee and I sleep together, and sometimes Lee and Crystal sleep together. Sometimes Crystal and I sleep together too, and other times one of us is sleeping with someone else outside of our marriage."

Richard's jaw drops. Doris shakes her head, but smiles. Another man I later learn is named Matt blushes profusely. Another man, his name is Darryl I will later learn and his name is the one on the auto repair sign nearby, spits out his coffee in a rather humorous manner. Lee just grins and shakes his head at me while the waitress takes a seat in the circle that has formed around me, and another man, his name is Tim, exclaims what they must have all been thinking, "What," before he catches himself.

Doris finally speaks up, and asks, "So you're saying it's not just the three of y'all?"

I watch Lee chuckling as he heads to the back room for kitchen supplies. "Sometimes it's not just the three of us, yes, that is right. The three of us are a union or marriage or trio – whatever term you prefer, but sometimes we like to date other people too, and in our relationship that is allowed as long as we all agree." Doris looks like she's going to faint, but luckily Tim has a question to keep the conversation going.

"So," Tim begins, "Is this like a gay thing or something?"

Chuckling, I say, "No. There are a lot of gay, lesbian, bi, asexual, and straight people who do this, and there are a lot of other people in each group who are monogamous so they only have one lover in life or at a time or even at all. There are even people who only do this – have multiple lovers – sometimes and not always. It really depends."

Richard interjects, "Do you think being, you know, the bi kind of gay is part of it?"

"Nope, but it might be. I honestly don't know, but for me, I think it would be the same if I had fallen in love with two women, two men, three or four of each, or two transgender people. I think it's more about loving and wanting multiple people, and doesn't have much to do with sexuality because people of all sexualities do this and others do not. The same way some people just feel best with one person, like a soul mate," a few of them nod, "We just feel better with more than one person, like a couple or a few soul mates."

"What do you do about jealousy," the waitress asks.

"You kind of have to either not feel it at all or you have to move past it. Some people just don't get jealous – they trust the people they love and want them to be happy with them and with anyone else. Some people get jealous at first, but then learn to see things differently because they want the people they love to have everything they need."

Matt says, "I don't think I could ever do that. I mean, doesn't it bother you when, you know, Lee or Crystal are together without you, or with like other people?"

Smiling, I say, "Nope. In fact, we all encourage each other to express ourselves in whatever way works best as long as it fits within our rules. I want Lee and Crystal to be happy, and I want that even if that meant they had to leave me tomorrow. They feel the same way, and so we focus on what each person in our relationship needs."

Standing by the grill, Lee says, "It's actually pretty simple. We don't see each other as belonging to us, but more as partners who choose each day to share our lives. We don't get to decide what the other does, and we don't want to. Instead, we share these experiences with each other whether or not any of us is involved at a given time."

"Exactly," I say taking a sip of my coffee. "We have our rules for our marriage, and we follow those rules, but the most important rules are that we trust, support, and take care of each other and our union first and foremost."

With a little hesitation, Doris asks, "What are the rules?"

Lee answers, "The rules can be anything the couple or trio or group comes up with. As long as the people agree on a set of rules, those are the rules for that relationship just like in your own marriage Doris. I'm sure you have rules about what you can and cannot do."

Doris nods, and I add, "In our case, we cannot sleep with anyone outside of our union without first talking it over as a family. We cannot lie or in any way deceive each other for any reason. If that happens, we have to work through it no matter how long it takes without any involvement from outsiders so our union remains strong. We must take precautions and only practice safe sex with any partners we have, and we cannot place the needs of others or ourselves individually over that of the union. If any of us start to do that, we have to revisit the union to decide if we want to remain together. We also require each other to talk about it – as soon as possible – if we feel anything is off, wrong, unbalanced, or unfair at any point. Finally, no one can ever be added to our marriage – officially or otherwise – without the agreement of all no matter how important the person becomes to any one of us. Those are our rules, but as Lee notes, rules can be anything people want."

Richard dives back in, "Do y'all, you know, do stuff as a group or just one on one?"

Laughing at the phrase "do stuff," I take a sip of my coffee and say, "Both. It really depends. Sometimes we want to all be together with or without others, and sometimes we want all three of us together. Other times, we look like shifting sets of couples where most things are one on one. It really just depends."

Nodding, Lee says, "It also shifts over time. When we first got together, Jackson and Crystal were inseparable, they started as a side experience for Crystal, and I was involved with both, but never with both at the same time or the same amount."

"That's right – when we were first together in Miami," I say.

Lee nods, and says, "And then we went through a period where the three of us were practically inseparable in all ways, and then we went through a time where I wanted a lot of time to myself and Jackson and Crystal were basically a couple and another time where Jackson and I were really close and Crystal was mostly dating someone else."

"And then remember that six-month period where I didn't want anything sexually? It was just the two of you then, and then Crystal had her own period like that too."

"Exactly," Lee says, "And then sometimes when an outsider is brought in for fun, that shifts dynamics in the household. So, really, it depends, and it changes depending on what we need."

"Well I'm going to say it because it has to be said," Tim says taking out a cigarette after putting his seat back at the table he took it from. "What y'all doin' sounds strange as all get out to me, I tell ya, and y'all should be careful because others will think even worse things than that round these parts. I won't go that far, like Chuck said with the gay thing, saying its wrong is damn hogwash cause what 'dem gays ever done to nobody, right? But, listen here good, not everybody around here is nice, hell some 'dem folks still hate ole Doris here for marrying that boy Danny just cause he black, so y'all be careful right? Somebody just had to says it, that's all I'm saying, watch out for assholes is what I'm sayin'." Everyone – including Lee and I – nod, and Tim shakes my hand and heads out to a blue truck.

Doris says, "Sadly, he's right y'all. It is strange, but it also seems good cause you got ole Lee here grinning and talking just like little Crys does all the time, so y'all just be smart and I'm sure it'll be alright. Hell, that's what Danny and I still have to do just in case – some folk are slow to adjust to new things round here."

Again, everyone nods around the little circle, and then the waitress says, "How does the bisexual thing work? Is it like being gay, but only sometimes?"

Laughing loud at the same time and probably both thinking about the "part time gays" t-shirt we saw at a Pride event years ago making fun of similar questions, Lee and I both say at the same time, "Not exactly."

"It's more like you see the world a bit differently," Lee says.

"Basically," I add, "We don't really care about genitals that much. Most people we've met that are gay, lesbian, or straight have a preference for this or that type of genitals, you know, though some of our asexual friends don't and others do. Anyhow, some like penises, some like vaginas, and some like specific body types as well. The same way some people want skinny or bigger, different hair colors, etc. For whatever reason, and I really don't know why to be honest with you, our brains don't seem to work that way. When I met Crystal, I wanted Crystal and I didn't care what was in her pants because I can do fun things with any of the options and same with Lee. You know, it's more about the person, at least for us, than anything else because we don't have the same genital preferences that other people seem to have. We can be with anyone, and even when they change sexes for one reason or another – like my college boyfriend did while we dated – it doesn't matter because that's not a determining factor for us. My college boyfriend, for example, was just as much of a man, just as beautiful to me and just as much fun even before and as his body changed from female to male."

"Damn," Lee says grinning, "You should write that down Jackson. That's exactly how I feel, but I never thought to explain it like that."

Laughing, I say, "I can't take credit for that. A lesbian activist and her bisexual wife taught me that when I was in college."

"So," Richard says pointing at me, "For you it's not about, um, genital, uh, stuff, you kind of like your own set and other types equally, is that it?"

"Pretty much, yeah, for me and a lot of people I've known, that's what the bi refers to – my body and bodies that look different from mine, but people define it in different ways than that too."

"Well, I'll be," Richard says shaking his head. "So, like, I can't imagine what I would do with, you know, male parts, parts like mine I guess, so that's the difference between us?"

"Pretty much, and I have friends who have male parts who have no interest in female parts and friends who have female parts and no interest in male parts, and that's the difference between you, me, and them in this regard."

"That's kind of fascinating," says Matt.

"I never thought of it like that," adds Doris.

"Do you think you were born bisexual," the waitress asks.

"I honestly don't know," I say putting milk into my fresh cup of coffee. "The same way I honestly don't know if people are born straight or gay or asexual or anything. I don't know if I was born poly or if others are born monogamous. I honestly don't know. I think it's possible that we are born these ways, but I think it's equally possible it develops as our brain develops. Either way, I know that I've felt this way as long as I can remember, and most straight, gay, asexual and other people I've talked to feel the same way. When I was in college in Houston, I had a professor, Dr. Mathers was their name I think, who pointed out that it shouldn't matter where it came from because in the end we could all treat each other well and have the same rights no matter how we became this or that type of person. I don't know what the answer might be, but I like that approach so I just try to be good to everyone."

"Pastor David would say that's what Jesus wants us to do," Darryl says speaking up for the first time, and Richard, Doris, Matt and the waitress all nodded. At the mention of the pastor, I think of the bookstore in Milledgeville and Lee turns back to the grill as if he's nervous for some reason. I wonder what that's about as Darryl continues, "It's that whole do unto others thing from the Bible. That's what it sounds like your professor was saying," and again everyone in the room nods.

The waitress, who I finally learn is named Shelby when Darryl and Doris tell her goodbye a few minutes later, comes back over and says, "What should you do if you think someone is a gay or a bisexual or a transgender?"

Smiling at the use of the term 'a' before the labels that I had only heard on television at that point, but would soon have to get used to, I say, "Generally, the best bet is to be a good friend to them like you would to anyone else. If you want to show them that you are a safe place, you can also start reading or watching things with gay or bisexual or asexual or trans people, and randomly mention such things. Often, we're looking for signs that someone might be okay to talk to, but generally, everyone has to come to things in their own way and should only talk about it when they're ready. So, just be a good friend and create a space where gay and bi and asexual and trans people are good and positive so if they are they might come to you when they're ready. Basically, demonstrate you care before you know for sure. That would be my advice. Lee?"

"Same here. I wouldn't try to push or talk to them about it until they come to you, but I would try to create the impression that you're a person they could come to one day."

Richard smiles and pats Shelby on the shoulder. Shelby nods her head, and goes to do side work. I watch as Lee works the grill, and continue chatting with Richard about the town, our lives, and other things. My first trip to Chuck's, I feel, has been a monumental success. Maybe I missed my calling as a sex educator working in small towns, I think, as I sip another cup of coffee and take in the surroundings that will become so familiar to me.

CHAPTER 10

Later that night, I was enjoying my experience at Chuck's and the unexpectedly fun conversations. Unfortunately, my spouses were trying to rain on my parade all night by reminding me that others in town would likely respond differently to my presence. Of course, I knew this. They knew I knew this. Like so many people who lived "different lifestyles," we spent our lives dealing with mostly negative reactions in person or when we turned on our televisions or news feeds each day. I knew they meant well, but I just wanted to soak up the positive moments for a little while that night. After I said about as much to them for the fifth time, Crystal left the house for a walk, and Lee went upstairs to read some book on religion.

It felt kind of odd being the positive, optimistic one in the relationship for once. Normally, I was the one pointing out all the bullshit, problems, and things we should be careful about when we dealt with new people. This time, however, they were the ones playing the heavy. They both seemed a little off, like something was on each of their minds that remained unspoken, since I'd gotten to town the day before, but I had no idea what was going on in either case. I was a little worried about them, and they seemed worried about me, but I felt like I was missing something.

I thought about the reactions to my presence in the diner that day, and wondered what it must have been like to have a Chuck and Thelma growing up. I remembered Crystal telling me about the night her parents learned she was attracted to girls, but I realized that I never thought to ask exactly how they found out in the first place. In any case, Crys remembered the night like it was still happening. She would smile so big as she told the story.

"They came into my room, and they said they knew about me and this other girl. They sat down on my bed, one on each side of me, and I thought I was in serious trouble. After a few seconds that felt like forever, mom said, 'You know there are going to be stupid people who think there is something wrong with you, but I know we raised you to be smarter than that.' I remember I felt like I started breathing again, and then dad said, 'You have to understand that other people can't define who you are little girl. You have to remember that you are just as good as anyone else, and that any man or woman would be lucky as all get out to be near you for even a few dag gone seconds.' I remember I started crying, mom put her arm around me, and dad patted me on the knee like he always did and said, 'Remember the sign kid, that's all you need to know.' We just sat there for a few minutes, and then they told me they loved me, and we all went to bed. It was just, I don't know, just what I needed to hear in some way that I don't think I even realized before then."

I thought about this series of events, relayed to me over too many glasses of wine so many years ago, as I stood in the den staring at "the sign" Chuck and Thelma taught their kids to base their lives on. It sat there, just above the record player Crys and Lee got me and maybe the only thing about the room they didn't change for my arrival, tacked to the wall as Crystal always said it had been. Simple wood, crude lettering, but thousands of memories captured in those words: "You are always becoming a better person than you imagine you are." I wondered how many times Chuck, Thelma and their three children stared at this sign in moments of turmoil, struggle, or sadness over the years.

It was in this very room, beneath this very sign, that Lee sat crying after the homecoming game his junior year of high school – almost exactly a year before Crys's chat with her parents about the girl they found out she had been dating in secret – because he thought he was going to hell. He was in love with some local boy that he, as of his drunken re-telling of this story on his birthday last year, still carried a bit of a torch for all these years later. He was scared, sad, and racked with the same guilt churches seemed to deal in all over the country. He was waiting for Crys to get home because he needed both his best friend and his girlfriend more than he ever had before, and that's when Thelma found him.

"I just blurted it out and I thought she was going to hit me or call my mom or something, and I wanted to pull it back in somehow, but she just hugged me while I cried. She told me about her cousin who liked boys when they were kids, and how the family basically disowned him except for her mama who found him a place to stay with a friend over in Louisville – another town near where we lived – and sent him food and money until he finished high school and joined the military. She said, 'No matter what happens Lee, you won't have to go all the way over to some other town because you'll always have a place to eat, sleep and be whoever you want to be here.' She told me to look at the sign, and remember that even Jesus said love was always a good thing and if anyone would know, she thought he would."

I tried to remember more of these two episodes, but only little details would come to mind. I remembered Crys being jealous of Lee for the next year because she was certain her parents would react differently if they knew about her until she experienced the opposite. I remember them finally stumping Chuck and Thelma when they explained to them, a few days before graduation, that they both actually liked boys and girls rather than one or the other. Although stumped, I remember being impressed that Chuck and Thelma responded just as positively to this news. I remember Crys did not like it when Lee talked about his first love, and Lee said this was okay because she had good reasons for not liking the guy. What I remembered most, even as I thought about these memories in the comfort of Chuck and Thelma's old home, was wondering what it must have been like to have that kind of experience coming out.

My own experience was an entirely different set of circumstances. The neighbors I lived with as a teenager after my parents died worked all the time so their two kids and I were always on our own. The three of us did not care for each other, but our moms had been close so we existed together in a shared space each waiting for the experience to end. In my senior year of high school, I would go down to the French Quarter with some friends, and we would look at the art, roam through the parks, and stand outside the bars listening to music. On one of these trips, one of the guys in the group and I went off on our own to hang out in this small alley off Carondelet Street where some older kids taught us to smoke pot the year before because he wanted to show me something.

When we got into the alley, the other guy, Mel, pulled out a magazine with pictures of naked guys in it, and showed it to me. I stared at the magazine in shock, and asked, 'So you like this kind of thing,' and he just shrugged. He lit a cigarette, and then held out the magazine with his left hand until I took it. I flipped through the pages, and as I did, I felt myself smiling and thinking about the one guy I had kissed at that point in my life one night on the river in the shadows. I didn't notice him move past me toward the exit of the alley, but when I looked up from the magazine, he was at the edge of the alley screaming, 'See I told y'all he was a faggot' to the rest of our group that had apparently followed us to learn the results of this experiment. I froze as the sounds of their laughter and derogatory terms swept over me, and dreaded the months before graduation.

Sometimes, in my sleep, I can still hear their voices laughing and taunting from the edge of that alley. The rest of high school was basically a series of beatings and responses to college applications that all still feels a bit like a blur in my head. All I really remember was a dedicated commitment to getting out of the city, and never coming back. I remember thinking, or hoping maybe, things would be different when I got to college, and in many ways they were. At the same time, neither the straight nor the gay students at my university took all too well to bisexuality or polyamory at the time so in many ways, except for when I was hanging out with River and his friends, I continued to exist somewhat hidden or in the face of continuous harassment throughout those four years as well. It wasn't until years later, when I stumbled into a group of poly and a group of bi people in Atlanta, that I started having any truly positive experiences with anyone I wasn't sleeping with. As a result, I always wondered what it might have been like to have a Chuck and Thelma.

As was often the case whenever I experienced the next very negative or positive reaction to my existence from strangers, I thought about all this that night listening to records in the den Lee and Crys made for me. I thought about the fact that Crys still ran into stories like hers, like mine, and many far better and far worse every year in her classrooms, and wondered if that would always be the case. I wondered just how many different ways our many Queer siblings within and beyond the acronym experienced the first times others became aware of their sexual, gender, or romantic differences, and held on to the fun I had in the diner that day.

I was thinking about all these things at once as I heard Crys say, "So what are you up to tonight?" She had just come back from her walk, and was still wearing the Eight Bells hoodie she got when we first saw that band in concert. She always said that hoodie calmed her in some way, and I wondered again what was going on with her since coming back to this town for that reunion. I thought about asking again, but decided instead to keep enjoying my happy day for a little while longer.

"Just listening to records and thinking about old times. How was your walk?"

"It was good. I just wanted to clear my head."

"You know I'm always here if you want to talk about it."

"I know babe, where's Lee?"

"He went upstairs to do some reading right after you left, and I haven't seen him since so I guess he's still up there reading or maybe sleeping by now."

"He's been tucked away reading a lot lately," she says running her finger across her lower lip as she often does when trying to figure out a puzzle. It reminded me of the time she tried to make sense of one of Deidre's projects, and we were all worried she would rub her lip all the way off her face. "I wonder what's on his mind."

"I don't know," I say, and then before I can stop myself, "The two of you both seem to have things on your mind you're not talking about since you got here."

Ignoring or somehow not noticing my implication, she says, "Yeah, we got a lot of memories in this place, I guess he's fine," while continuing to rub her lip. "Do you know what he's reading?"

"He said it was some religious stuff, and it looked like pamphlets and a couple books when he was going through his bag earlier, but otherwise, nope, no clue."

She stares at the sign for a few minutes, continues to rub her lip, and says, "It's probably nothing, just curiosity I bet." After over a decade together, I am fully aware that the look on her face does not match the nonchalant words she is saying. I really feel like I'm missing something, and it is starting to bug me as she says, "I think I'm going to go on up to bed. Yep, I think a good night's sleep is just what this doctor ordered." She walks over to me, plants a soft kiss on my cheek, and heads upstairs. I tell her goodnight, but I also notice that her lips trembled a little bit as they reached my face. I watch her make her way up the stairs before turning back to look at the sign and picking up my journal.

Crys is taking late night walks. Lee is reading about religions. Both seem nervous or worried about something. This all started with them returning to Queens. What does this mean? What is going on? What am I missing? I write these words in my journal, and stare at them for a while. Nothing comes to mind, and after a few minutes, I put on another record – Pat Benatar's *Live from Earth* – and start reading over character sketches I created while I was still in Tampa, which I'm hoping might be the start to another book. Outside, Queens is quiet and I find myself looking forward to exploring more of the town in the morning.

CHAPTER 11

"You're that fella that shacked up with Chuck's kid, aren't you," an older man asks me as I stand in line at the coffee shop downtown. After a couple days enjoying the regulars of Chuck's, I decided to venture out into town. The coffee shop is on the other side of Queens Boulevard, and appears to be doing well based on the number of people in the shop at lunchtime. It has more than we do by a wide margin, and I wonder if that's normal or a more recent change. On either side of it, there are cafes that serve lunch and dinner, and this place seems to serve as the place people hang out in between meals.

"Yes sir, I think that would be me," I say turning to look at the guy. He looks like he might be in his sixties, and is a wearing a shirt that seeks to teach us that Savannah is beautiful. He probably picked it up from one of the novelty shops every beach town seems to have lining its most tourist friendly areas. I'm expecting him to say something else, but instead, he simply shakes his head, grunts in an odd way, and then walks past me out the door of the shop. I'm guessing he doesn't want to be friends with me.

"Don't mind ole Harold," the barista says as I reach the front of the line, "He's just, you know, a little old fashioned and we don't get a lot of people like you 'round here." I'm sure she doesn't mean people in long term committed loving relationships, but I place my coffee order and try to let the subject rest. I feel eyes on me the whole time I'm at the counter. Every time I look around, the faces move and find something else to stare at, but they're not very good at subtlety from what I can tell. Maybe the subtle hateful stare is a trick only taught in cities, I wonder as the barista hands me my beverage and tells me about a lovely outdoor seating area I might like down the block. There were three people served before me that did not get this information with their orders, and I want to believe she is simply offering suggestions to someone new to town even though I suspect that's not what led to this suggestion. I'm tempted to camp out at a table in the middle of the place all day just to watch the barista and silent-stare-people squirm, but I didn't bring anything to read or write so I'm sure I'd get bored. I make a note to do this another day.

As I step back out onto the sidewalk, I see ole Harold pointing in my direction as he talks to a couple of other older men – though not as old as him from the look of them – in what appears to be an agitated manner. Remembering the record store is in that direction, I stand there for a second wondering if I'm in any danger. Sadly, this is not an unfamiliar exercise in my life. I have learned that the world is full of New Orleans alleys. In the end, I decide I'm probably fine in broad daylight in this small town, and head for the record shop. I pass by ole Harold and his posse – as I think of them– and all of them greet me with angry looks as if I'd stolen their cars. No one says anything to me, and I figure I can handle dirty looks as well as anyone else if that's all this will be.

I stroll past a couple thrift shops on the way to the record store, and stop to look at some clothes in the windows. A lot of the stuff looks like fashion from my childhood, and I wonder how the 80's and 90's became so popular again. As I'm standing looking at a pair of what I'm almost certain are Hammer parachute pants, a lady walks by with her little girl, and as they approach, she pulls the girl close to her. She shoots me an angry look, covers her kid's eyes, and I'm reminded of a friend of mine in Tampa who was told he "should be ashamed" of himself when a little girl asked him where he got his skirt and her mother found this question unsavory. After a couple days with the regulars at Chuck's – even amidst the stares of other patrons who came in each day – I realize with a bit of an ache just how familiar I am with looks like the one I'm getting from this lady.

"You gonna get a lot of that 'round here boy," an older black man with a white beard says from a doorway two shops down. He is wearing a Carhart work shirt, and smoking a cigarette while watching the street. "You get used to it, but you never really accept it, know what I mean?" I smile knowing exactly what he means, and sure he's had as much or likely even more experience with this kind of stuff as I have over the years. In his case, I was willing to bet the harassment came without anyone having to tell people about him ahead of time. "Names Sylus, I run this here shop, and I been dealing with people like that in this here town all my life. Hope you got thick skin boy, cause you gonna need it being all married to two people and one of them a fella." I nodded. He nodded. He threw out his cigarette, and said, "Why don't you come on in here for a minute, got something I want to show you."

Although it said School Supply on the sign and there were in fact school supplies in the very front of the shop, the bulk of the place housed various types of greeting cards, gospel tracks, lyric sheets, posters, chapbooks of various sorts, and in the back, so many journals. "Your wife said you would need these when you got here," he said pointing to the journals.

"My wife was right as usual," I said with a chuckle.

Sylus smiled and leafed through a couple of the journals, "Yeah, she was always a good kid. Her pops and I were friends, even back when that was not a smart idea around here, and I remember that little girl digging through these racks to find the perfect notebook. She would sit and listen to mama's stories all day long, and help us out when we were cleaning the place up. My mama always had a thing for that little girl." He stares at the walls, and a picture of a beautiful middle-aged black woman on one wall standing by a lake notebook in one hand and waving with the other. He explained that his mama opened this shop in the 80's after his dad passed away – "first black owned business on this strip that I know of" – because she had always been fascinated with paper and art. "My parents, they saved for years for this place, and so after she was gone, I decided to run it myself."

We talked for another twenty minutes, and over the next few months, I found myself coming back to see Sylus for little chats. I would pick us both up coffees from down the street, and spend a couple hours with him working and chatting in the shop before going to look at records. That day, however, the main thing on my mind was the story about Crystal. I knew nothing about it before he told me. She never mentioned a paper shop, Sylus, his mother, or anything else related to the place. It was a piece of her childhood that was wholly new to me, and I wondered how many other pieces I might find while I lived in this town. I also found it odd that Sylus didn't, "Know much about Lee, you see, I don't think I ever saw him that much, except as just another kid roaming around the town and later working part time at Chuck's, until he started running Chuck's a couple months ago." In my head and from their stories, I always imagined the two of them as basically inseparable since they were kids, but now I wondered if there was more to that story as well.

A couple blocks from Sylus' shop, the record store stood calling my name. If there was anywhere in this town I was going to feel like I fit, I guessed it was either the record store or the bookstore. Those were two of the very few things I had trouble imagining my life without. As I approached the shop, three young kids, teenagers I guessed, were looking through the records on the table outside marked one dollar. Two of them looked like mirror images of each other, and the third was pretty obviously related as well based on similarities in their faces. I figured they must be siblings, and wondered if the two mirror images were twins. When they saw me, one of them – I would learn her name was April and she was looking at the one dollar CD's on the other outdoor table – squealed and said, "Oh my god, you're Jackson aren't you? You've got to be him because you're new and Jackson is the new one."

I was starting to get used to this either infamous or famous thing, and I just smiled, nodded, and waved. April walked up to me, and excitedly shook my hand as she began talking faster than should have been possible, "Oh my, we heard about you, oh my, you're adorable too, are you really a writer? How did you become a writer, oh, where are my manners, I'm April and these are my sisters May and June." May and June waved and I stood there puzzled by the names and the fact that I thought I was looking at two sisters and a brother before she spoke. I stared at the one called May for a second, and thought about seeing River for the boy he would later become the first time we met even though his bodily transition had not started yet. I wondered if May was similar or just preferred to look more boyish while April took what I would learn was a rare breath.

"We were actually born in October, but mom like, really, like, loves the spring and summer so she named us that way, isn't it weird? I mean not like weird like you are, but still kind of odd, we're a little bit different like you're a lot different, you know? What am I saying, you know all about being weird don't you, oh my, you probably know more about that than I do, yep, that's probably right, so wait, you really date both Mr. Lee and Ms. Crystal? What is that like, is it fun, how do you do that, are you planning to pick one someday, oh my…" She continued for another six minutes – I timed her wondering how she had so much energy and lung capacity – until her sister, June, finally put an end to the ramble.

"She gets a little excited." April blushed and smiled.

"I can see that."

"You're just so different," April blurts out, and June pats her on the shoulder and nods.

"Well, April," I say and she nods, "I'll answer any question you have, but you might have to catch me somewhere I can sit down and you might need to slow down to wait for answers."

She giggled, and June mouthed thank you. "Okay, uh, I can come by Chuck's and talk to you, yeah, I can do that, well, I could do that, but I…" She was about to start going again, but June caught her and she just smiled.

"That sounds fun April. Come by anytime, and same for y'all two." May never says a word, and after a few more minutes of back and forth and one more ramble from April about the differences in weights for vinyl records – the kid knows her stuff I think in the midst of this one – June looks at her watch, and says they need to go. The whole time June wears a smile, and May simply stares at me, drops her head blushing, and stares at me again.

As they walked away, I went into the shop. Along the wall on the left side as I entered, there was a selection of new vinyl records spanning the length of the shop and arranged alphabetically without genre markers. I liked this place already. The counter was on the other side of me as I walked in and took up the front of the store all the way to the right side of the shop. In front of the counter, there was an open area with a couple chairs, and behind that, the place was arranged in rows that mirrored the one against the left wall. There was a little sign that said, "We don't believe in genres or other forms of segregation – all vinyl organized alphabetically." In the back of the room, I could see a couple of CD racks set up, but this was, by far, mostly a vinyl place and I felt at home almost instantly.

I was enjoying the Prince record playing on the stereo and looking through the first bin, which contained new vinyl marked down for clearance, when I heard a voice coming from the back of the shop and moving in my direction. "Did you enjoy the stooges?"

Turning around and meeting eyes with a young woman, maybe 27 at most I thought, with soft blonde hair, a big grin, a vivid tattoo of a rose on her left arm, and a Yeah Yeah Yeahs t-shirt with the sleeves cut off, I said, "I've never been all that interested in punk music, well, except for Patti Smith and Against Me. I don't know, does Sonic Youth count as punk?"

Laughing, she says, "No, I meant the calendar you were talking to outside, or as I call them, my own little Three Stooges."

"Oh," I say thinking the nickname is kind of fitting and wondering why I didn't come up with it myself, "Yeah, they were fine. The one named April can sure talk."

"Yes, she can. She doesn't even really need anything to say beyond hello, and she's off to the races. She's smart though, that one, and likely going places. They come by here almost every day because their mom sets them free after their school or housework is done and their dad is obsessed with the goofy greeting cards Sylus sells at his shop, it's the one that says school supply on the sign."

"Yeah, I met Sylus a little earlier. I'm pretty sure I'm going to spend a fortune on his journals however long I'm here."

"That's right. I think I heard you were a writer from somewhere down in Florida. You'll enjoy the stooges a lot," she chuckles, "June is kind of the leader and she keeps April in check, but May is different, kind of keeps to herself and doesn't say much. She comes in here and spends hours listening to records and chatting one on one, but when the other two are around it's like she's a mute."

"Seems like an interesting bunch, and I have a feeling April will give my ears a workout while I'm in town."

"So, Mr. writer, do you ever do any plays?"

"Plays? No, at least not yet. I enjoy going to plays, but have not yet had the urge to try my hand at that skill just yet. Why?"

"I'm involved in the very little theatre we have in this town, and so I was curious. So, you just a collector or do you need some musical expertise?"

"I'm just looking around, but I never mind conversation while I look."

"Works for me," she says moving behind the counter, switching out the Prince record for the Dolly Parton one she had when she came from the back of the shop. "How is the adjustment to Queens going so far?"

"It's kind of strange, but overall good I guess," I say flipping past Green Day albums in the G section of the new vinyl. "Everyone knows who I am, and everyone is very curious about me and about my family. Some people are nice about it, and others pretty much hate me already, which is kind of what I expected. I don't know, only been a few days, but so far it's kind of strange, but kind of okay too, if that makes any sense."

"Sounds about right to me. I remember when I first moved here it was a bit of a culture shock, and I came from a town about the same size. Queens is just so much more interconnected than my town was, you know, like everyone knows everyone and everyone finds out about everything, which isn't true but that's how it feels most of the time. Sylus was my first friend here, and I would go out with him and his wife and their son, and people stared at me like I was destroying their world. Hell, they got it worse than I did, and it was just so strange. I feel for you."

"So, you're not from here? Why did you end up here?"

"You say it like it's a prison sentence," she says sorting a few – I'm guessing – newly arrived albums. An image of Chuck in a warden's outfit floats through my mind.

"Okay, true, I have my own bias here."

"I actually chose this place believe it or not. I grew up over in South Carolina, a little town called Clearwater about the same size as this one, and I liked living in a small town. While I was in college in Augusta, where Chuck wanted your wife to go, you know, I got into music with local bands and a couple people doing stuff with records. I enjoyed the arts and music at college, but I missed small town life.

At the same time, I didn't want to go back to Clearwater where all my family and most of my high school friends still are so I started looking at other towns. I was talking to a kid I grew up with about the record store boom that was happening at the time in relation to the Record Store Day holidays and stuff like that, and I thought, that would be a fun job. So, I put together my savings, some money my grandmother left me, and with the help of my friend Cat who knew someone in banking, I got a loan to open a shop. When I was looking at small towns, I liked Louisville, but then I found this place and the price to start up was cheaper than other places. I thought, what the hell, and here I am four years later the music source for the town."

"Wow," I say, "That actually sounds pretty cool. So, is it a fun job?"

"It has its ups and downs. Playing with the music, introducing music to people, and chatting with casual customers and collectors like yourself is a lot of fun. At the same time, it takes a lot of work and I spend a lot of time in creepy places looking at record collections for sale. Like the other day, to give you an example, I was out at this warehouse in Wrens where this guy had all this great 80's pop, and then I'm out there all alone hoping I'm safe and I spend three hours picking out stuff and then I make my offer, and the asshole decides not to sell because he – you know everyone thinks they're an expert – believes his stuff is worth way more than it is. Stuff like that just sucks, but no one sees that side of the business."

"Yeah, that does not sound fun, and I admit I never thought about that side of things even though I practically live in record stores." I find a Rolling Stones album I've been looking for, and check its condition. It looks good, and I move toward the counter saying, "You said Chuck wanted Crystal to go to college in Augusta?"

"That's right. There is a little, though bigger now, college over there and Chuck always wanted his kids to go there. None of them did. I don't know much about the other two, probably a question for Ruby, but Crystal had the grades and everything but chose to leave for Florida instead. Chuck was proud of her, but I remember him taking a liking to me almost immediately because I went to his dream school."

"Who is Ruby?"

"Oh yeah, after a while you forget that new people don't know everyone yet," she chuckles and rings up my record, "Ruby is like the unofficial town historian around here. If there is something to know, no matter how big or small, Ruby knows it and might even have pictures of it. She lives out by the lumber yard, and spends most days out on her porch watching her great-grandkids and other kids in the neighborhood play in her yard, but she knows pretty much everything about this place because even now she seems to have sources all over the town."

"I should probably talk to Ruby. I studied this place a lot before getting here, but I could never find out where the name came from in the first place. Do you know?"

"Why it's called Queens? Come to think of it, no, I don't know that either. If anyone would know, Ruby would I'm sure of it."

At that, I pay for my record, tell her I look forward to our next meeting, and head out of the record shop. The sun feels good on my face as I look up at the sky for a few seconds. When my gaze returns to the town in front of me, I see people across the street whispering and glancing in my direction. I walk the rest of the shops on this side of the road, and then cross the street. When I cross the street, the whispering group disperses, and I can't help but wonder what exactly they might be saying about me and my lifestyle. The rest of the shops hold little interest for me, but I enjoy the walk back to Queens Boulevard, and then further to Chuck's where I go inside to kiss my husband and enjoy a burger with my wife.

CHAPTER 12

A couple months after my first trips to the school supply and record stores, I finish cleaning up my novel – a love story about two girls who grow up together in Apalachicola before running off to Chicago to open a bookstore specializing in LGBT works that doesn't go exactly as they planned. I'm only about 10 percent happy with the finished project, which is how I know it's ready. For some reason, the more certain I become that a given project is useless the more other people seem to enjoy it. I can't pretend to understand this, but it works. Stealing one of Crys' smokes from the kitchen counter, I go out on the back porch with my laptop and turn in the manuscript.

As I have always done when I finish a project, I take a stroll in the moonlight, and think about the work, what might be next, and whether or not I'll get to keep doing this for a meager living. The neighborhood is so quiet at night. There are very few lights, even on Main Street itself, and it has an eerie feeling I associate with the calm of the beach at night and the weighted silences in horror films right before someone gets the ax. When I first got here, the quiet bothered me. It still does, but that feeling is lessening each night, and I figure Lee is right that I won't notice it once I've been here for a while. As I walk past the house on the corner of 2nd Ave, I hear dogs barking and the sound of an automated sprinkler system turning on in the distance. I keep walking and before I even notice it, I'm at Queens Boulevard looking at a gas station I didn't realize was open 24 hours.

I spent three months living in Chicago figuring out the details the young couple would see in their daily lives. I rode the trains because they couldn't afford cars. I spent time at lesbian and bisexual book clubs – always with the permission of the regulars – because they needed to understand their customers. I searched real estate listings and neighborhoods to figure out that they lived in an area called Pilsen that was starting to gentrify, but still was mostly a working-class minority neighborhood populated by families and students at the nearby university. There was something about roaming around places – whether small towns like Queens or big cities like Chicago – that always ignited my own creative process.

I purchased the first pack of smokes I had bought since I finished my last novel at the gas station. Like walking through my neighborhood – in Tampa before, but now here – this was a ritual I created long ago. Other than bad days where I usually only had a couple before throwing away the rest, it was the only time I allowed myself to purchase smokes, and enjoy a whole pack. I decided it might be nice to stay in the neighborhoods instead of moving up to Main Street like I had been doing so far. I crossed Queens, and found myself walking past houses that looked almost exactly like the one I lived in on the other side of the boulevard. I lit a smoke, hit the button on my ear buds to re-start the Pink Floyd album I was listening to, and kept walking while breathing in the silence.

The latest novel arose entirely by accident just like the first two. I was driving back from Long Beach, Mississippi, a small town I sometimes liked to go to for a few days to write when I was having trouble ever since I heard Bob Dylan's "Mississippi" and decided to check out the state, and my car broke down without warning. I had been taking highway 98 along the coast to enjoy the scenery, and I found myself stranded in a place called Port St. Joe. Luckily, the place had a couple auto shops, and so I spent time sipping coffee at a shop off 98. While I was there, I met a young woman on the way to meet up with her secret high school girlfriend in Chicago. As she talked about life in that area growing up and their plans, I felt the first organic urge to write I experienced in months.

As I strolled through the neighborhood on the other side of the boulevard that night, I came across a cemetery that I had not yet noticed. I saw it just barely, thinking it was a park at the time, about two blocks further back from Main Street as I walked through an intersection a few blocks past Queens Boulevard. I decided to check it out. I have always had a fascination with parks, and I was thinking this might be a new place for me to think and journal. As I got closer to the place, I realized it was not a park, but I also saw something or someone moving on the edge of the space. I was about a block away, but I could see the shift in the shadows when whatever it was moved.

They seemed to be swaying back and forth, and then they fell to their knees. I decided it was a someone over there in the cemetery in the middle of the night. Stephen King would be proud, I thought, and kept walking hoping I didn't startle whoever it was.

Earlier in the day, Lee came bouncing into my little den having finished the novel. Crys had finished it weeks before, and already given me detailed notes I would ignore as usual. "This may be your best one yet babe," Lee said taking a seat beside me, "I really like the way you blended the past and present throughout the narrative, it was kind of fun." I thanked Lee, and he stared up at the sign for a minute. "Could you do me a, I guess, research, favor?"

"What you need babe," I said thinking this would be easy. One thing I enjoyed more than most was studying anything that came across my path. I even helped Crys with her projects occasionally when she didn't have extra funding for a research assistant. I would dig through archives with her, read transcripts of the oral history interviews she collected, and make little notes in the margins just in case they were helpful. Before I left Tampa, I had a stack of these transcripts in my bedroom that I was supposed to read in search of patterns as part of Crys' latest project. I wondered what would happen to that project now.

"I was wondering if you could look into that gay church they got over in Augusta, and maybe other gay churches too. I don't know, kind of see what they're about I guess."

"Sure babe, that will actually be very easy and you could probably do it without my help. Most of what you'll find is easily gathered on the internet these days."

He nodded, but said, "Probably, but I don't want to miss anything that might be important."

"Okay, so, what exactly are you looking for?"

"How about just give me anything that looks interesting so I can read it and think about it. I have a few thoughts, but I'm not sure I want to talk about them yet." Okay, I thought, this is Lee trying to tell me what's going on with him before he is ready to talk about it. He had done stuff like this for years. Something would be on his mind, whether minimal or huge mind you, and he would be quiet and distant.

Then, when I would notice the distance, he would suddenly want help with something he didn't need help for at all. A few weeks or months later, I would learn that the "something" he wanted help with was part of whatever was making him distant or quiet when he finally started talking to me, Crys, or both of us about it.

"Works for me, but I'm here when you do want to talk about wherever this latest obsession with religion is babe. I might never be religious, but if you want to be I hope you know I – and I'm sure Crys too – will support you in any way we can."

Lee didn't say anything else. He just nodded, sat there quietly for a few more minutes, and then headed out to the kitchen to start the dinner he planned to celebrate me finishing my editing process. The three of us did have a nice dinner a couple hours after Lee came into the den and a few hours before I stood by the cemetery that night. After dinner, I handed Lee everything I found on the churches, and reminded him again I was always around if needed. The whole search only took about twenty minutes, and as I had suspected, he could have done it with no help. He went upstairs, and like every other night lately, buried himself in information about religion. I was standing on the corner of another intersection thinking about these events when the person at the cemetery started walking away from it into the neighborhood. At first, I was glad I was going to have the place to myself, but then, I noticed the purple headband the person was wearing as it caught the light and they disappeared onto one of the other streets in the neighborhood.

I was still too far away to make out much, especially with my weak eyes that led Lee to keep suggesting I needed glasses, but I knew that headband. I bought that headband. Lee and I came up with the design of that headband. It was handmade by a local artist in West Palm Beach, Florida at the flea market on the edge of that town. We went there for vacation one year, and Crys fell in love with the accessories and designs of that artist, Lauren Alberts, I think that was her name. Lee and I asked her if she could make one in purple with initials woven into it for Crys while Crys was getting a cup of coffee from the stand down the aisle. The lady said she could, and we exchanged contact information. A few weeks later I drove out to West Palm Beach to pick it up, and Lee and I gave it to Crystal on her birthday later that year. What was Crys doing in a cemetery in the middle of the night?

She had been taking walks every single night since I got to town, and according to Lee, she had been doing that since the reunion. In fact, Lee mentioned that she always did that whenever they visited Queens. When I asked him about it, he said I should talk to her, but his eyes said he thought he might know the answer. When I asked her about it, she said it was a long story, and refused to elaborate even a little bit. I played these conversations back through my mind as I headed for the spot I thought she was standing in at a faster pace. Was she coming here every night? If so, what was bringing her here each night, and why didn't she want to talk about it? I barely noticed much of the cemetery as I moved through the tombstones looking for wherever she was standing when I first saw her without realizing it was her.

When I got to about where I thought she was standing, I started looking around for anything that might be informative. The grounds were very well kept, and there were about twelve tombstones in this area. For a second, I thought about the very real possibility that Chuck and Thelma were buried somewhere around here. Was she visiting them, I wondered, and if so why not talk about it? I was scanning the tombstones thinking this was useless when I noticed the exact type of tulip Crys grew at Chuck's place – and back in Tampa and back in Miami now that I thought about it – sitting in front of one of the stones. It was clearly cut only recently, and sat there like a beacon drawing my attention. I looked around me, but I was completely alone. On the stone in front of me, the etching said:

Autumn Matthews
1981 – 1998
Beloved daughter, sister, and child of God
Remembered in love 'til the river runs dry

Who was Autumn Matthews, I wondered standing there reading the text. Who was she to Crys? The dates seemed relevant. She died the same year Crys and Lee graduated from high school, and the same school year Lee was captain of the team and Crys was homecoming queen. She was born the same year I was, the year after they were. They must have grown up together, I thought, but I never heard either of them mention this person even once. I flipped through all the names of the people Lee mentioned from childhood, and did the same with the few Crys mentioned over the years. Nope, no Autumn on the list. No Matthews either. Were they friends? Were they more than friends? Who was Autumn Matthews and why was Crys visiting her grave in the middle of the night?

I had no answers. The questions kept swirling in my head alongside the feeling I was missing something that plagued me since I got to this town. My first impulse was to go find Crys, and ask her about it. The last couple weeks, however, suggested this was not the best plan of action. For whatever reason, this was something Crys was keeping extra private, and I didn't want to violate her right to do so. Then, I thought I might ask Lee who Autumn was, but again, this seemed like a bad idea because he had always played Crys' Queens stuff very quiet, and there was no way he could know I was figuring things out and not give that away in his interactions with her. What made him especially fun for Marcus on poker nights also made him a terrible place to store secrets of any kind – a fact he demonstrated all too well over the years. I thought about the town's newspaper, and the online archive. Maybe I would do some digging on my own first. After all, there was no way for me to know this was where Crys kept going. I tried to tell myself it might be just a random coincidence.

I couldn't think of anything else as I headed back to the house that night. Between Lee's religious awakening and Crys' midnight walks, something was going on or maybe a few things, and the uncertainty was really starting to bother me. It's a funny thing that happens after spending over a decade living with the same people, you get used to their habits, mannerisms, and other little characteristics. You learn that your husband craves cartoons when he is stressed out. You notice that your wife's accent gets deeper when she's very happy or very sad. You get used to the way your wife blows on her coffee in the morning even though it's already poured over ice. You become familiar with your husband's tendency to lose towels after carrying them to random places throughout the house because an idea struck him in the shower. You also know when your husband and wife seem upset, off, worried, or just somehow different from the people you are used to spending your time with. This is what had happened in my house, and more and more I was beginning to think it was more than just the change of scenery at fault. "What have you done to us Chuck," I asked the sky in a whispered plea.

When I got home that night, they were both already asleep. As I checked in on each of them, enjoying the sight of them at peace and relaxed, it hit me that I couldn't remember the last time the three of us slept in the same bed or the last time the two of them did. I did, however, remember that these events last occurred in Tampa. In fact, I realized that the two of them were spending very little time together – just the two of them – at all these days. Our relationship had always been somewhat fluid, and our sleeping arrangements regularly shifted over the years for shorter and longer periods of time. This was probably why I had not noticed the shift before now. Part of the freedom we gave each other involved a lot of shifts, changes, and adjustments. At the same time, something felt different this time. It was almost like there was some unspoken disagreement taking place between them that I could feel even though I couldn't quite understand.

CHAPTER 13

My curiosity – or maybe the newfound surplus of nicotine in my system – wouldn't let me sleep. I tried at first, not long after getting home from my walk, but I kept seeing the tombstone in my head and wondering who the person was. While my family slept upstairs, I went out on the back porch with my laptop, smokes, and coffee to do some digging. I reminded myself of "dissertation Crys" years ago on the balcony in Miami sitting up all night cursing at the screen of her computer and asking Lee and I why she went to graduate school in the first place. I thought about why we ended up in Queens in the first place, and spent a few minutes cursing Chuck just in case his ghost was around to hear me.

I didn't find much. I didn't know if that was because of the time-period – she died as Google arrived on the scene. It might have been the limited published information about small town events. It might have been that there wasn't anything to find beyond the obituary and couple mentions of the name related to high school events that I read multiple times that night. According to the obituary, she died – no reason or cause listed – on a Saturday in March of 1998. She was survived by a brother who she was inseparable from for most of her life, and her two parents – the preacher of the Baptist Church and his wife Louise. I thought about finding some pictures of them, but I was too focused on trying to understand who she was and what she might have meant to Crys. There was information about a memorial service, and the text explained that she loved poetry, dancing, Jesus, and animals. She was a junior in high school at the time, a year behind her brother – Lee and Crystal too I thought – and planning to go to college in Thomasville. That was it. I didn't have much more than I started with as I stared at my screen in the early morning hours.

The mention of Thomasville reminded me that Lee and Crystal considered going to the college there before deciding on Florida State University about an hour south in Tallahassee. In many ways, this often felt like where Crys' life began based on what she did and did not talk about. They arrived in Tallahassee for school in the fall of 1998, and spent the next four years living right near the campus in an old motel that had been converted into apartments. It was in their first week of school that they decided to leave the closets behind, and live openly as a bisexual couple and people who dated outside their own coupling. Lee majored in communications with a focus on journalism, and even wrote some pieces for the school newspaper and some pamphlets put out by members of the arts community that existed in the space between Florida State and Florida A&M. Crystal dove into the study of history – and especially women's history – and excelled in the program.

I remembered their many stories of the place, and the time we all went up there to see Deidre speak. The place had changed a lot since their days at the university, but it had a certain charm for them as a turning point in their lives. Crystal talked about sitting at Lake Ella and imagining the black Christian baptisms that started the place in the 1800's when it was called Bull pond, and the days where the cottages that now held novelty shops were honeymoon suites. Lee talked about hanging out at the capital with activists and other journalism students seeking to catch the next big story, and the thrill he got when the campus turned into a football fan club every weekend each fall. This same thrill annoyed quite a few other people who thought school should be about education first and foremost, he would explain. They talked about roaming the downtown area of Thomasville right across the Georgia border whenever they got homesick or stopped on their way to and from visits to Queens.

As the morning emerged and the town sounded like it was starting to wake up, I grabbed my bag and headed for the library. I figured any information I couldn't find online would be in the library or just not available. For a moment, I thought about Ruby, the town's resident expert, and wondered if I should pay her a visit. The library was on the same side of Queens Boulevard we lived on. It stood on the corner of 6th and Main, and stared across the street at the local bookstore I still had not managed to try after hearing Lisa and Crystal express concerns about the place. The library was a little building that looked like most of the other storefronts, and it was usually deserted except for children's activities and occasional book clubs from what I could tell. The only exception, as one of the regulars at Chuck's told me, was a girl named Samantha who, along with her best friend May, practically lived at the place because she loved books and her mom worked all the time.

The library wasn't all that helpful either in this case. I found a few old yearbooks, and a couple pictures of Autumn from events, but that was it. There wasn't anything else about who she was, how she died, or how she might be connected to Crystal beyond being classmates in different years of high school. I was trying to think of a connection based on what I knew so far when I remembered that Autumn had a brother who was a preacher's son and Lee had been in love with a preacher's son in high school. Was this person the same person, I wondered as the librarian approached me. "Excuse me, Jackson," she said, and I nodded, and she said, "Maybe I could help if you're looking for something specific in the town records?"

She was a tiny brunette who looked to be around the same age I was, and occasionally came by Chuck's with a women's history or reproductive rights book in hand. She would order a coffee and a piece of pie before reading her book while moving her lips silently in rhythm to words on the page. Lee said her name was Kate Dixon, and she came from somewhere out in Texas, but moved here in her late twenties from Atlanta when the previous librarian, Miss Ruby, retired. No one knew much about her, and most people figured she wouldn't stay long because she kept to herself. However, the local bookstore owner had developed a significant bit of hatred for her. Everyone in town was waiting for the two of them – the local and the Texan as they put it – to end up in a brawl on Main Street over what determined a "quality" book or a woman's moral options concerning reproduction. They were sure it would be a fun fight to watch. The only other thing I knew about her was that Shelby said to never go to a restaurant she recommended unless I wanted to get sick, but I had not bothered to find out what story might exist behind this warning.

"Sure, I'm not having much luck on my own," I say with a chuckle, "Do you know anything or have any information on a kid named Autumn Matthews that died here in the 1990's? All I could find was the obituary, some old yearbooks, and a few mentions and photos over the years."

"Hmm, I don't know if I can help you there," she says pushing a strand of hair out of her eyes, "I've only been here about two years so I'm still kind of an outsider to town business. You would probably have better luck talking to Miss Ruby out by the lumberyard. I don't know if you've heard of her yet, but she's kind of the historian and used to run this place. Wait a minute," she says and walks over to a corner in the back of the library for a few minutes. When she comes back, she says, "Yeah, Miss Ruby is your best bet. Samantha hasn't even heard the name before, and she's basically in training as the future Ruby if you ask me."

"Yeah, um, the lady at the record shop, I just realized I haven't caught her name yet, that's probably bad, anyway, she suggested Ruby for another question I had."

Laughing, "The names will come, you're just new. Yeah, Lacey, the record shop owner, is close with Miss Ruby and lives out there on that side of town. Yeah, Ruby is probably your best bet unless you want to talk to the brother."

"Autumn's brother? Is he still in the area?"

Chuckling and smacking her knee, she says, "Wow, you are new to town." She smiles, "Ooh, thanks, I needed a good laugh today. There is only one Matthews family in this area, and they are about as well-known as your own Chuck and Thelma and Ms. Ruby. They founded and still run the big Baptist Church in town, right up the road down there across from the AME." She points at the obituary I'm still holding, and says, "Based on the time, I would say that she was fourth generation, and that would mean the brother mentioned would be our own Pastor David. So, you might want to be careful talking to him because of, you know, your family and such, but he might be the best source available on this one."

"Huh, I didn't know the pastor's last name. I haven't run across him yet."

"Well, he's out of town right now and has been since before you got here, I think. He does these mission things or workshops every year where he travels to Augusta, Atlanta, and little towns like

Possibilities and Cordele in South Georgia and other parts of the southeast to help folks and pray, I think, but even so, you might not meet him because he doesn't come to Chuck's at all, and he certainly won't now I bet."

"Why doesn't he come to Chuck's?" I might have been new, but even I knew this sounded odd, well, at least it did before we took over the place.

"Chuck hated the guy is the rumor I heard, but I don't know for sure. From what I heard, he was the only person unwelcome other than the idiot racist folks that live out past the lake and ride all over town with their Confederate shit. I actually have wondered what he had to do to earn that distinction, but I have no clue."

"Why did you say he certainly would not come now?"

"His wife. She is not a fan of the," puts her hands up as quotation marks, "alternative lifestyles" if you catch my drift. Her and Jenny, the lady that runs the bookstore, and some of the other ladies at that church are like the morality squad in this town. We had this young couple, open, out, nice folks raising a kid, but they moved away right before you got here." I remember Crystal mentioning another out family, but had not heard anything about them since. "Well, I was talking to them, they were like my first real friends here, before they left, and they were telling me how Linda, that's Pastor David's wife, and her friends basically made their lives hell in a bunch of little ways and expressed concern about a "kid like theirs." I heard later at Chuck's that this wasn't the first time, and after my own experiences with Jenny, I can't say I'm surprised."

"What happened with Jenny?"

Laughing, she says, "Well, I mentioned that I worked with non-profits to get women reproductive access and resources while I was in college the first time her and I chatted out there on the street, and the next thing I know I start getting all these pro-life and family values pamphlets here at the library and at my house all the time. Ever since then, her polite interest from that first chat is basically gone, and she kind of just stares at me."

"But I heard Pastor David was kind of liberal and okay with people like me?"

"Oh, he is, and even works with support groups and stuff for Christians who are trying to learn how to accept and love themselves as, you know, LGBT people. He would probably love you, most likely, but his wife and most of his church are a whole other story. The flock does not always agree with or completely follow the shepherd is the way my daddy would put it. I think that they probably just see that "LGBT stuff" – as I've heard Linda say – as David's little hobby or something. They're also good at being polite while still hating people. They'll just say bless you or bless your heart when they don't like something."

I suddenly realized a lot of people in town said that to me, and I thought that meant they liked me. I remembered telling Crystal this and her just laughing uncontrollably and having to tell Lee who also thought it was hilarious. That damn little prankster had gotten me again. Were all those people just making fun of me or trying to be polite or something? I felt both stupid and annoyed at the same time. Somehow, this was also Chuck's fault in my mind, but bless his heart, I thought and chuckled. It was a handy phrase. "So, I might get some information from him, but I should steer clear of his wife and her little crew?"

"Yep, that would be smart." She shook her head as if to say, 'what are you going to do right,' and we both laughed. For a second, she reminded me of a woman named Tasha I dated in Miami who accidently shaped my life more than anyone else I could think of. She had the same piercing eyes, and when she laughed she shrugged her shoulders at the same time the way Tasha did. As we said goodbye, and I left the library, I found myself wondering what ever happened to Tasha and if she still hated Crystal and me.

We were out at a concert in Northern Miami. I had been seeing Tasha for six months, and I was having a good time but also sure the relationship's expiration date was approaching – six months was already the longest ongoing affair in my life other than River. Tasha had also been dating some snooty professor lady who lived down in Coral Gables, and she wanted us to meet. I know it sounds terrible, but I only went because the concert was out of my budget – I mean could I really miss the chance to see the Roots live in a small club venue, come on, that was a no brainer – and Tasha was paying. I was standing at the bar enjoying the music and ignoring the dancing in other parts of the overly cold building when I felt a tap on my shoulder. I turned around, and saw Crystal for the first time.

We didn't tell Tasha we were leaving. We didn't make any plans. I didn't know Lee existed. We didn't talk about much at all that night come to think of it. It was all a blur. We were at the bar somehow mesmerized. We were at a little coffee shop she liked off NW 138th Street. We were at my apartment and she was on the balcony talking on the phone – with Lee, I now know. We were still wrapped up in each other a couple days later when she had to go back to work and home for fresh clothes. We were both new to the city, and I got lost the first time I met her intentionally later that week for drinks. She had come from Tallahassee, and I had come from Atlanta, and she lived with a guy named Lee that I would have to meet at some point because their lives were "complicated." Neither of us ever spoke to Tasha again, but in a nicotine, alcohol and lust filled spring we did receive many angry messages from her.

Three months later, Crystal sat me down and told me all the details about the guy named Lee I had been hanging out with from time to time while we dated. I was curious, and so we all went out together a couple times, and then Lee and I spent some quality time together on the Egyptian cotton sheets at their townhouse. The next couple months became an ongoing three-way interaction in most respects, and at the end of the summer we all moved in together and began living as we still did 12 years later. From Miami to Tampa to Queens, it was hard to believe it had been over a decade since I forgot about a cute laugh amidst shrugging shoulders when I met a girl in a Guns N Roses t-shirt whose voice sounded like music.

I was thinking about these things as I decided to walk into the bookstore for the first time. It was just a basic, sparsely decorated room with Christian posters on the walls and shelves of used books that looked like they had been there without adjustment since the store opened at the end of the eighties. There was a lady in a red sweater sitting beside the counter who looked at me in a way I was sure could inflict harm in some galaxy, and another lady with a similar look in her eyes putting books on the shelves and humming what I thought might be a Kenny Chesney song. Neither of them looked happy with my arrival, and I wondered if this was a bad idea. "May I help you," the lady shelving books asked.

"I'm new in town, and just figured I would see what the book supply looked like."

"Well, that's alright, but you should know I don't really carry your kind of books here."

I thought about saying something like, 'what, no Billie Letts at all,' but I was sure she wouldn't appreciate the joke. I bet Billie Letts would appreciate the joke. "I'm not sure what you mean," is what I said instead.

"We are a Christian store, and so we don't really do alternative stories here. I only carry more family friendly and wholesome types of stories," she said while shelving a battered copy of Stephen King's *It*. I couldn't help it, the statement and the book in her hand together made me start giggling and I couldn't stop.

"I don't know what you find so funny, Jackson," she said and I realized that she knew how to turn my name into a curse word. Maybe Crystal learned that here.

Smiling and kind of enjoying this, I said, "I'm sorry, I just never thought of *It* as a wholesome, family friendly type book." She just stared at me. Then she shared a look with the other lady, and both shook their heads. Was this a silent 'Bless your heart' I wondered. "Well," I said, "I guess I'll be going then since it seems like you don't think you have anything to sell me." They continued staring at me, and I wondered exactly how much fun it might be to be a fly on the wall of this shop five minutes after I left. I left the shop, and headed toward Chuck's to process the events of the day, the pieces of information I gleaned from Kate, and a few pieces of pie I suddenly felt calling my name in a very loud voice.

CHAPTER 14

The next morning, I was sitting at Chuck's drinking coffee and enjoying – by my count – my thirteenth chat with May. Interestingly to me at the time, April had never shown up to chat and neither had June, but May became one of my most frequent companions. May would later tell me I became her new favorite person because I was a fountain of information, and didn't look at her funny for the way she dressed or acted. I would tell her that I had a similar reaction because she reminded me of my first love back in college. I don't know, even now, how much time we spent together, but there was just something that always felt like family or somehow special about May.

We also had a lot in common. She had dreams of being a writer, and lots of questions about LGBT groups and history. She was especially curious about transgender people. She would show up at Chuck's and even at the house loaded with a surplus of questions about these topics, and we would chat for a couple of hours before she left with more books and information. She was a senior in high school who felt like she never quite fit either between April and June or within Queens. She was also about to turn 18 and graduate early so she was trying to figure out her next steps. I was surprised how much she reminded me of a better version of my younger self, and had already made some calls to some of Crys' friends to get more information about colleges and scholarships.

As we discussed the short story she'd been working on about a young girl who worshipped caterpillars and dreamed of being a butterfly, Lee arrived at Chuck's asking if I wanted to take a ride with him. I knew he was headed over to Augusta to get some supplies for the restaurant, but I thought Crys was going with him. Apparently, the plans had changed, and he wanted to know if I was interested in keeping him company. "We'll be back tonight," he said, "And I'm sure you've been itching to get out of town since you got here." I wasn't itching yet, but even I was surprised by this. So far, the town was surprisingly interesting, and I was still trying to figure out what was going on with Lee and Crystal and planning to meet and hopefully have a chat with Ruby at some point.

To get to Augusta, we hopped on Highway 1 just beyond the edge of the town, and followed it past towns called Wrens and Blythe until it became Deans Bridge Road around the edge of Augusta. The drive only took about an hour, and after we passed the military base, we slid under the Bobby Jones Expressway and entered the city. At some point, we turned off Deans Bridge onto a road called Wrightsboro and followed this to the location of the restaurant supply store. It turned out we weren't picking anything up, but rather, again adjusting the orders for Chuck's that would be delivered in the coming months.

Business was still down, but Lee wasn't worried about it. He was, however, worried about a fight he had with Crystal that morning. When I asked what they were fighting about, he only offered vague responses, and said Crys was in a mood. "You two seem to be having issues ever since I got here, what is going on?"

Sighing heavily, Lee said, "We're fine Jackson," there was the version of my name that I was sure translated into a synonym for stupid. "You know how things go, sometimes you're closer, sometimes not so much. We're just adjusting to being back home, and it brings up stuff."

"Like what?"

"Nothing for you to worry about babe," he says in the dismissive way I am starting to hate. They both keep saying nothing is wrong or it's no big deal, but that is not how it feels. "Sometimes Crys just can't let go of stuff, and so it gets a little tense. It's always been this way, you know." Yes, they had always fought from time to time, but it was never like this. They barely seemed to speak or touch at all, and the tension was all over the place this time.

"It feels different this time Lee, I'm worried about y'all."

Lee didn't respond. He just kept driving, and we made our way into and through the city. After he finished talking to the people at the supply store and around the time I ran out of rocks to kick in the parking lot, he said he wanted to check something out. I said okay, and we headed back down Wrightsboro toward downtown. I saw a sign for the local university, and mentioned that I heard Chuck wanted Crys to go there. I made a mental note that I might like to check the place out at some point. This part of the city looked more like a small town, with residences and independent shops lining the road on both sides, and I wondered how many of the people we passed had ever been to Queens.

"Yeah, that was his big dream. I don't know if we've ever talked much about the family, but Crys' siblings were, to put it mildly, kind of fucks up in the end, and so she became the symbol of hope for his childhood dream of going to that school. We applied to it, and both of us got in, but we decided to leave the area. Chuck wasn't happy with that, but he was supportive."

"Why didn't y'all want to go there?"

Sighing again and looking off into the distance without realizing the light had just turned green until I pointed it out, he said, "It just seemed too close to Queens after all that happened when we were teenagers, and we just kind of both wanted a fresh start. I don't know, at the time, I think Crys just needed to be as far away from Queens as possible, and I wanted to be there for and with her. I visited the campus and thought about it, but she didn't even bother. In the end, we just decided it wouldn't work, and we left. I don't think either of us ever thought we would live in this area again."

Lee went quiet, and a few minutes later we were parked in front of a church. I looked at Lee, and he said, "I want to talk to some folks here about some things. You don't have to come in if you don't want to." I didn't want to come in. Even a church that liked people like us was still a church and thus not for me. "There is an independent book store I heard about 1 block up," he pointed in the direction in front of us, "and a few blocks that way," he pointed the way we came. "It's called the Book Tavern, and there's also a record store over there and a coffee shop called New Moon, I think," he said with a look on his face that told me he planned this, and was hoping I would be okay killing some time while he got all Holy.

"Sounds good, I'll take a walk," I said grabbing his hand, "Unless you feel like you need me in there with you." Thankfully, he didn't need that, and I disappeared down the block as he went inside the church. I hoped he would find whatever he needed in there, and wondered if his newfound interest in religion had anything to with his issues with Crys of late. I didn't know, and I had a new place to explore so I put it out of my mind. I walked up the street, and saw a lot of people milling around in front of both occupied and vacant stores spanning what looked like about seven or eight blocks.

I spent the next couple hours roaming around the downtown area. I found the record store Lee mentioned first, and leafed through the vinyl that was, for some reason, separated not only into genres but also based on the artists' country of origin. I didn't find anything I wanted that day, but made a mental note to check the place out again in the future. I was hungry so I walked to the next block, and found both the bookstore and a coffee shop next door to it. I ate a muffin and enjoyed some coffee. It was nice to be in a room full of strangers again, and so I just sat there thinking and reading for a while soaking in the anonymity I used to take for granted. I wondered about Tampa, and if I would be there again.

When I finally tired of the coffee shop, I went next door to the Book Tavern. It was a two-story space with an outdoor seating area. The proprietor appeared to be a man a few years older than me who had a beard that seemed to fit the rustic, academic feel of the shop. He was behind a desk debating local politics with a couple other people. The shop had a surprisingly diverse collection of literary, popular, classic, and niche fiction works blended with a rather large – especially for the size of the space – collection of non-fiction works on politics, the environment, and religions. I didn't go upstairs, but I did spend half an hour with the fiction shelves. Yes, I was looking for one of my novels. In fact, I found one for sale.

I noticed something that would have annoyed the hell out of Crystal – a book she recently bought was much cheaper here – and wondered what she was doing. I left the shop and sent her a text just to check in, but I didn't get a response. I walked around downtown for a while longer, and stopped for a few minutes at another coffee shop that looked more like a bar for a mocha. There was a blonde singer on the stage in the front performing an acoustic cover of a Neko Case song Crystal liked. I was thinking about going up another block when I finally heard back from Lee. I headed back to the church to see how he was doing and what we were up to next. I made a note that Augusta might be a good place to come on the days I did get an itch to get away from Queens.

When we finally got back in the car and headed toward Queens, Lee had another stack of pamphlets to study. He was smiling and humming as he drove so I asked him what it was like at the church. "It was really nice," he said, "And they had lots of information, which is what I wanted. I met a nice guy, about our age, from the area and his husband Lenny, and he told me the church basically saved his life when he was a teenager. He said his parents caught him in bed with another guy when he was a teenager and sent him to one of those so-called treatment places. He was totally messed up afterwards, who wouldn't be right, and then he found this place and they helped him make sense of everything. I can't recall his name, but he introduced me to the current pastor, and they gave me all these materials and a full schedule of events. It was nice."

"So, are you becoming religious now?"

"You know, I think I always was kind of religious, I mean, you know I always believed there was something out there." This was true, but the addition of churches into the equation was new. "I don't know if I'm becoming religious so much, it's more like I just got more interested in it when we moved up here again, like I was when I was a kid."

"Does this have anything to do with a son of a preacher man?"

"Maybe," he says, his voice softer than a moment ago.

"Is he still in the area?"

"Yeah," he says, softly again. The change in voice is curious to me at the time. "But I haven't seen him yet. I just know he's still around, and doing well from what I've heard."

"Are we thinking of rekindling the old flame?"

"I don't know," he says in that same soft tone. "I really don't know, it's, well, it's complicated and we haven't seen each other or even spoken since my second year in Tallahassee. I don't know, I'm not sure how that would work."

Nodding, "Well, I love you and if you want to pursue it I'll be here for you. Just make sure I don't have to deal with any fire and damnation type stuff."

"Deal," he says.

We pass the expressway, and the country look and feel I'm getting used to starts to take over my view again. I'm starting to think Lee's drunken ramblings not so long ago were accurate. He's got it bad for this guy, whoever he is, and then I wonder if it's David Matthews. I realize that I'm selectively guessing here since there are so many churches in our town and the other nearby towns. At the same time, I wonder about it. I even think about asking him, but I'm kind of surprised he has talked about it this much today and I don't want to push. I wonder what Pastor David's wife and her friends would say about a rekindling. I wonder if they know about Lee. Lee just stares off into space as he drives the same way he does a lot now. We are mostly silent as we pass through Blythe, Wrens, and the countryside while the sky grows dark with pending night.

CHAPTER 15

The next morning on the back porch I saw Crystal for the first time since I left for Chuck's the morning before. She came outside as I was reading an email, and said, "I really need to get out of town Jacks, you want to take a ride?" Wondering again what was going on between her and Lee, I said sure. She lit a smoke, smiled at me, and said, "Good, let's go to that book store in Milledgeville you liked, and maybe get some lunch while we're out there." I nodded, she smoked, and I put my stuff in my bag on the table. Once she finished her smoke, she said let's go, and we hopped in the car.

Crys didn't speak the whole way over to Milledgeville. Instead, she blared her favorite Ryan Adams album, picked at her lip, and responded to my initial two conversation attempts with short, clipped answers. She was obviously angry, but not at me. I wondered what the fight yesterday had been about, and I remembered that she hadn't been home when we got back from Augusta. I wondered if she had gone out to the cemetery again, or if that was just a one-time thing I used my imagination to turn into something much more interesting. I was aware, and my spouses often reminded me, of my tendency to do this at times when I wasn't writing. When we stopped in Sandersville to use the restrooms, she asked if I wanted anything to drink, but otherwise it was like taking a country drive with a mute.

When we got to Milledgeville, we went to a place called the Velvet Elvis Grille and Tap for lunch. It was a cute restaurant that looked like the type of place that would make locals proud and tourists empty their wallets. Crys said she wanted to try their raspberry dressing, and I was in the mood for a sandwich. As we sat down, she said, "Your husband is a pain in my ass sometimes." I always loved how my name became a curse word when she was mad at me, and Lee became "my husband" whenever she was mad at him.

"Do tell," I said with a smile.

Sighing just like my pain in the ass husband, she said, "Ugh, I don't know. He's just really getting on my damn nerves lately. It reminds me of when we first started hanging out, and I kept feeling like I wanted to throw him through a wall all the damn time. I don't know, I'm just annoyed, don't pay any attention to me, I just needed to get away from him today."

"I don't think y'all ever told me how you started hanging out. I think I just assumed you were attached at birth or something."

"Ha! No, I hated him and the feeling was mutual when we were kids. He was an arrogant little church boy, and I was the weird artsy girl. We didn't start hanging out until our friendship groups collided the first year of high school. Even then, I kind of mostly thought of him as the annoying jock I would likely murder at some point." I have trouble imagining Lee as an arrogant anything, and I still sometimes forget my docile, peacemaker husband was once a big-time jock. "We were kind of like that, enemies stuck with each other thanks to friends and my dad's place, until the homecoming game sophomore year when we kissed on a dare at a party after the game. It was surreal, I thought I was going to puke, but it was a dare. So, anyhow, we kissed, and something changed that night, and we've been annoying each other ever since." In all honesty, that was an accurate description of a lot of their interactions. "Since coming here again, he's just really bugging me more than usual. I love him, but I also kind of want to beat him up sometimes, I don't know."

"You two do seem kind of estranged these days. It's been like that, in my opinion, since I arrived at least."

"It's probably no big deal," she says sighing again. "You know how it is, like when you and I fight or when y'all do, it'll pass. I don't want you to worry about it, I just need a place to vent and you're usually good at that."

"It's a talent I've worked hard to perfect. Also, let's be honest, it's kind of nice on the rare occasion when I'm not the problem," I say smiling at her.

Laughing, she says, "Yes you have and yes it is. Strange too, but it happens I guess." She laughs a little harder, "So, on a more fun subject, have you met the librarian yet? She comes into the diner sometimes to read, and grew up somewhere in Texas or something?"

"Yes, I have. Did she remind you of Tasha?"

"Oh my god, she so reminds me of Tasha! She's a little prettier to my eyes, you know, but has the same mannerisms and smartass sense of humor. I've been hanging out with her at the diner the last few weeks sometimes when she comes in – well after she finishes her reading – and I kept thinking y'all had to meet because she's so much fun."

"I had the same thought. She's one of the fun people in town in my head along with Sylus, May, Lacey, and the regulars at Chuck's."

"Same here," she says as our food arrives. We have a lovely lunch, and spend most of it making fun of and enjoying town gossip. I realize with a bit of sadness that we don't have as many of these chats since I came to town. Her and Lee are obviously having some issues, but I feel like they're both a little distant from me as well. As she does her best impression of Jenny, good enough that I almost choke on a fry and wish I recorded it to show to Kate, I realize that I miss these moments and how common they were before we came here. I find myself hoping they are both right that this is just another transitional moment in our lives, and blaming Chuck for my loss.

After lunch, we go to the bookshop that was once a firehouse, and enter to the sounds of Emmylou Harris' *Profile II*. I giggle because this album is one of my favorites, and one that annoys Crys because she can't stand Harris' voice. She punches me in the arm, and says, "You didn't call Lisa so you could prank me, did you?"

"I did not," I say wishing I would have thought of that.

Chuckling, she says, "Damn, I would have been kind of proud if you had."

The shop is empty, and we do not even see Lisa when we arrive. Crystal starts flipping through some of the books on a table with a sign that says, "History Comes Alive," and I make my way over to the fiction section to get the Richard Russo book I promised myself last time I was in the shop. After a few minutes, Lisa comes walking in from what must be a back room, and says, "Well, isn't this a lovely surprise," and gives both of us hello hugs and an offer of coffee we both accept. I guess her and Crys moved past the handshake hello stage as well, and I wonder if Crys has been back here since I got to town. We all sit down at one of the tables in the shop, and Lisa says, "So has the news reached Queens yet?"

"What news," Crystal asks as she blows on her coffee, ice cubes in the coffee, or both.

"They say we're in for more lightning storms this year. They're saying it'll be big ones like in the eighties, and that we should take precautions."

"They say that from time to time, but it's never a big deal," Crys says. "The ones when I was a kid were so scary, and caused so much damage that I think it scared everyone into taking every sign of a storm way too seriously."

"I don't know. A lot of the folks here are really worried."

Feeling confused, I say, "I don't see what the big deal is?"

"That's because you didn't grow up around here Jacks. We don't get hurricanes or things like that, but the lightning storms and the droughts scare people about the same way."

"Yeah, people get really worried about it," Lisa adds, "And there is some real damage some years even though nothing like the storms in the eighties since I've been here."

"Huh, learn something new every day. I just never thought all that much about lightning, maybe I got spoiled living in Tampa."

Crys laughs, and says, "Yeah, we've been to the lightning capital so I guess it's different for us than for the folks up here." I remember reading somewhere we lived in the lightning capital of the nation when I was in Tampa, and now that I think about it, we did see a whole lot of lightning each year. I'd never paid much attention to it except for the first time I saw a strand of it standing from the ground to the sky. That was strange and unsettling, but after a while, kind of like the quiet here, I got used to it.

"I guess so," Lisa says, "But around here it's the talk of the town. Although, I guess maybe y'all are too busy welcoming the prodigal son home over in Queens."

"What do you mean," I ask suddenly curious.

"Oh, y'all just don't pay much attention over there do you," Lisa says with a laugh, and then continues, "Ole Pastor David is back from his trip. His wife was in here the other week talking about how glad she was for him to be home."

"Ah, nope, didn't hear he was back, and I haven't met him so I wouldn't know if I saw him around town." Crystal looks annoyed, and excuses herself to go to the restroom. I find myself wondering if this has to do with his sister Autumn. "I did hear that I should steer clear of his wife, but otherwise nothing."

"Is she okay," Lisa asks gesturing to the bathroom.

"I think so, she has been working through some things."

"She just looked pale for a minute there," Lisa says and tugs on a strand of her hair. "Anyway, whoever told you that might be right. When she was in here the other day, she mentioned y'all, and I was kind of shocked."

"What do you mean?"

"Well, especially as open minded as David seems to be and with all the stuff she loves to read, I would have thought she didn't have any problem with folks like y'all. But when she was in here, she told me Queens was just going to hell, and explained that Chuck's had been taken over by some perverts. She was like, 'It was bad enough with that strange liberal old man, but now it's just a shame the people running it have no morals.' I was surprised, and thought about calling y'all, but I figured it was probably just talk."

Crystal came back from the bathroom, and took her seat beside us. Lisa turned to her, "I was just telling Jackson that Linda, you know David's wife, was in here with her panties in a bunch about the three of y'all taking over Chuck's."

Crystal nodded, and said, "It's not surprising. She has never kept it secret how she feels about people like us and our LGT cousins She thinks we're all a bunch of trash or something. Luckily, they don't ever come to the diner and we have no use for the church so we're not likely to run into each other much."

"There are people in Queens that don't go into the diner?"

"Business has actually been down a lot since we took over and brought Jacks up here, so now there are quite a few who apparently don't want to come by. At the same time, there have always been folks who didn't like the diner – or really, my mom and dad – so they didn't come by. Mom and dad were too close to the black folks for some people and too liberal for some others. Their support of Lee and I after we visited in college and told everyone we were bi alienated some other folks too. It's a small town, and old hatreds die hard, you know. And then, there were a few people dad or mom turned away or didn't like that weren't allowed at the place, but that was not often – I only know of four myself and of course, mom's blanket ban on the people who are always spouting the racist junk. They always told us it wasn't worth staying open if they had to jeopardize their values. It's the same thing now, and since Jacks and I both have nice incomes and Lee has plenty of savings, we're not worried about the restaurant. It makes enough money to keep the doors open, and we don't really need more than that right now and the regulars are very loyal."

I wonder why she doesn't mention that David is one of the ones Chuck did not like, but I follow her lead and keep quiet about that detail too. "Wow, I never knew any of that," Lisa says, and then adds, "But I get it, I've had similar issues and things since I opened this place. I was telling him I was so surprised by Linda because she loves the erotica and other sexual books I carry, and even loved Jackson's novels."

"Just because she loves the stories doesn't mean she loves the people, I guess," Crystal says once again adopting the faraway look her and Lee both keep having these days.

"I wonder what her friend Jenny would think about her preferred reading materials," I say and all three of us share a good laugh. "I mean, after all, she doesn't carry that alternative stuff because she's a Christian business."

As the laughter dies down, Lisa says, "Okay, I would have paid money to be in the shop when you were there. I bet she almost had a heart attack when you walked in."

"I said the same thing," says Crystal, "And ole Barb was there that day too, based on Jacks' description, and she might be the most close-minded of the whole group."

"I have this image of them washing the place from top to bottom just in case they caught something from you, and doing a kind of prayer circle to cleanse the place after you left," Lisa says.

Crystal adds, "My favorite part was the family friendly speech while holding a horror novel, I mean, a great novel, but still a horror story," and proceeds to the tell the story in full to a very grateful Lisa. "I kind of want you to go back just to get some more fodder for our conversations Jacks," Crystal says with a big smile.

"I might pay for that too," Lisa says getting up to refill her coffee.

"Maybe I could get a shirt that says W.W.J.D. on it, and has Jackson going down the shirt from the J, and then wear a big cross and carry a pink Bible with me. I could do my hair like Tammy Wynette, and we could create our own *Sordid Lives* sequel in town," I add.

Spitting out her coffee and echoing Crys' loud gaping laughs, Lisa says, "You know I always did admire Brother Boy."

"We all did," Crys says with a smile, and again I think that for just these few minutes Crys seems like herself again. She is laughing, chatting, and matching any kind of witty banter that comes along. She looks relaxed and peaceful like she always did before we moved to Queens. More than ever, I'm sure there is something going on and I need to figure out what it is and how I can help her and Lee. In the meantime, we spend the rest of the afternoon hanging out with Lisa, and we leave with my new novel, a couple history texts for Crys, and a couple books that I think will be helpful for May.

CHAPTER 16

"I was wondering when you would make your way out to see me young man," Ruby says as I walk up to her porch about a month after our trip to Milledgeville. I found her exactly how everyone seemed to know her, sitting on her front porch swing, sipping sweet tea, and smiling. There were no kids in the yard today, but I knew that could change at any minute. Rocking back and forth in a slow rhythmic fashion, Ruby looked like a queen awaiting the arrival of would be jesters. I got the impression that she could outsmart us all, even Crys and maybe even Deidre. She had a sense of authority that just flowed from her short gray hair, wrapped around the dark skin that held her body together, "black beauty wrinkles and all" as she would say, down to a pair of feet that always tapped exactly in line with the drum beat of whatever song was playing on a radio she kept in the window. She waved or motioned with the longest fingers I had ever seen, and spoke deliberately with a voice that suggested more than her fair share of cigarettes over the years.

"Was it a foregone conclusion already," I asked as she motioned for me to join her on the swing. As I sat down, she chuckled and slapped her knee. As quickly and easily as she moved and spoke, it was hard to remember she was over halfway through her eighth decade.

"Come on now child, how often does someone come to town married to both a homecoming queen and a captain of the football team? It would have been down right discourteous if I didn't get to meet you at some point."

Chuckling, I say, "Well, it is a pleasure to meet you Miss Ruby. You are quite the legend in this town." Ruby was born in Queens on the – at the time and in some ways still – black side of town just as the depression hit the country. The youngest daughter of parents who worked on the farms surrounding the town, she grew up running in the streets, painting with the skill of a much older person, and singing in the AME Church. At the age of 20, she was immortalized in film throwing a tomato at a white police officer who was beating a little black boy. The next year, she birthed a little girl who would become the first in the family to attend college in Atlanta, and who would create a law firm that specialized in civil rights litigation. Even in old photos, she was slight of build and full of power.

"You can just call me Ruby, it was good enough for my mama, its good enough for me, but it means I get to call you Jackson too," she says with a smile, and I nod. "You know, I actually knew about you before you came to Queens." In the 1960's, Ruby was a guest at Chuck and Thelma's wedding, and one of the first people to have a meal when Chuck's opened – an event that some people still cited to explain why some folk in town never liked Thelma and Chuck. She was approaching her fourth decade on the planet in May of 1970 when she led a carload of friends to participate in the walk through Augusta to protest the jail conditions and death of a black teenager, which would devolve into the Augusta race riots when white police responded to marchers with unnecessary force. Later, she made her living working in the Queens library until finally handing it over to Kate, and selling her own art on the side.

"Wow, maybe you do really know everything," I said with a smile, and Ruby just laughed. In the 1980's, Ruby led the coalition of black church families that helped the town recover from the damage the lightning did to the – at the time wholly white – Baptist church, and rallied many of the white families she helped during the rebuilding process after the AME church burned a few years later. She also served with Chuck, Thelma, David Matthew's parents, and other town leaders on the board that investigated the electrical problems that caused the destruction of the AME church in the first place. Like Chuck, Ruby was basically a fixture in the town and a part of most of its major events.

"No, I don't, but some of the more superstitious folk around here seem to think so," she chuckles again, an infectious laugh, and sips her tea. "You know some of them have already come by here trying to find out what kind of damage the lightning might do this year like I'm some kind of psychic. Hell, I see the same news reports they do. My mama always said folk would believe anything, you see, if you just kept a little bit of mystery around yourself."

"So then how did you know about me?"

"My little girl, she lives up in Atlanta, is quite a fan of your books, and I'm sure you'll be all too happy to give me some autographed copies I can surprise her with later."

"You are correct, and I'll go one step further and meet up with her if she ever wants to."

"That's a good boy." She smiles and waves to a group of children moving through the neighborhood. "Will you look at that Jackson, not too long ago a multicolored group like that would have caused a lot more trouble than it does these days." I nod, and she continues, "Kind of funny how our country has basically not come very far and come very far at the same time don't you think?"

Thinking about May telling me how Miss Ruby explained the importance of the Black Lives Matter movement to her and her friends, I nod, and say, "That's the way it seems." As the – sadly history showed always present and never fixed – killings of people of color escalated again in the country a few years back, Ruby had taken it upon herself to have talks at the library and in the schools when invited to explain the movements that had risen in response. Like other parts of the country, media reports on the issues often carried more than just a little bit of racism and attempts to paint the movement, like other movements for racial justice in the past, in a rather negative light. Ruby shook her head after sharing these details with me that day. I couldn't think of a better response, and wondered if real change would ever come.

We sat silently for a few minutes, and then she said, "So, are you just here to hang out with an old lady, or are you hoping to learn something?"

"I'm always hoping to learn something," I say and she howls with laughter and nods her head, "Do you know anything about a girl named Autumn Matthews that lived here in the 1990's?"

"I probably know as much as anyone else, but that ain't much. She was a quiet kid, very smart and always had her head in a book. She was the younger of the two children Preacher Joe and his wife Louise had, the other one was her brother David who is the pastor of the big church now. I think your husband and wife might have been the only friends she had other than David, but I don't remember little Lee being all that close to her. The four of them spent a lot of time together in high school, and I often thought her death might have been the reason they moved off to Florida."

"How did she die?"

"She killed herself honey, it was very sad. It was her junior year, so the year your family graduated, and she had been at the high school with the rest of them until the middle of that semester, right after the homecoming game, which, I'm sure you noticed, is still a big deal here. Afterwards, she was homeschooled, and nobody saw her that much. She was always so shy and quiet to begin with, you see, and so it was like she disappeared until we finally heard about her death. My guess is that little girl was going through something tough, but I've never heard what it was and I would guess only David or maybe Crystal would know."

"Not Lee?"

"Well, Lee wasn't really friends with Autumn I don't think, like I said, not all that close it seemed, you see, he was friends with David and then Autumn and Crystal were friends, you see. In high school, Autumn and David leaned on each other, and that's kind of when the four of them started all hanging out together. Then, Lee and Crystal got close at some point, but I never heard of him being all that close to Autumn back then, you see, so I don't know what he might know about all this. Maybe he was, but I didn't hear about it. Why are you so interested in all this stuff?"

"I don't really know. Lee and Crystal have been acting odd since we moved here, and I came across her name and thought maybe she had something to do with it somehow."

"Maybe, maybe," she rubs the side of her face and looks up for a minute. "It might also be pressure or family obligation type stuff because Crystal was supposed to be the kid that got it right after the other two, and she did, but her leaving was really hard on the town and even more so that Lee left too. It was the same way when my little girl left for a lot of folk in town, but I always knew she was doing the right thing, she was always too big for this place and maybe Crystal and Lee were too. But it was different with them, especially with David also leaving to go to Bible College in South Carolina, it was kind of like the stars of that high school class just all kind of disappeared at once."

"I've thought about that too, but I just don't understand why that pressure would be so intense after all these years." Like many people in town, Ruby was aware of the failures and disappointments of Chuck and Thelma's first two attempts to mate. The oldest, born in late 1970, was named Jakob and never met a law he didn't break. By the time he reached high school, he had already been arrested for stealing, fighting, drugs, and even beating up a black girl in town. He didn't finish high school, but instead ran away to Augusta on his 16th birthday with some other guys. Chuck and Thelma did not hear from him again until they went to the Augusta morgue to identify his body three years later. He had been in an altercation with another guy over some debt, and the guy shot him in the chest at point blank range.

"Well, part of it is small towns Jackson, and part of it is that by the time Crystal was a teenager she basically represented the last chance for all of her parents hopes and dreams. Professionally, she, I think, eclipsed anything any of us ever imagined, but she didn't stay and become a leader in the town, she didn't want children, she showed no interest in taking over the restaurant, she came out as bisexual which most folk in town still don't understand, and she rarely came back to town. I would guess that all these things hit her when her mom died, and hit her even harder when Chuck died."

Crystal's other sibling looked like the opposite of her big brother for most of his life. He was born on a stormy night in 1972 – two years after big brother and eight years before little sister. He made the highest marks in every class, played sports with passion and sportsmanship, and demonstrated an incredible ability with musical instruments. He went to events at both the AME and Baptist churches, and even worked for Ruby at the library sometimes. He was popular and well-liked by the whole town right up until the day he got his first car. It was his sixteenth birthday, and he headed out on the highway toward Louisville to see a girl he fell in love with at camp the year before. No one ever knew exactly what happened, but he ended up leaving the road at some point and losing a game of chicken with an old oak tree. There was still a small white cross on the tree that marked the encounter all these years later. One year before their trip to the morgue in Augusta, Thelma and Chuck buried their middle child in the family plot that sat in the back corner of the cemetery where I had seen Crystal.

Finishing off her sweet tea, or at least that glass of it, Ruby continued, "Now, Lee is another story. He wasn't much to write home about aside from his athletic skills until he started hanging out with Crystal. He was kind of a shy kid who often got in trouble in stupid ways, but thanks to the influence of David's family, nothing all that bad ever happened and his minor transgressions were forgiven. See, he was the pride of the church in some ways because of his sports stuff, you see, and they kind of looked after him and kept him from any real trouble when he was kid. Crystal kind of took him under her wing at some point in high school, and suddenly his grades, outlook, and personality seemed to change overnight. He became a better and better kid as high school went on, and maybe coming back here is reminding him of those times both good and bad in ways that are hard for him."

"You make a lot of sense," I say because I can't think of anything else. I know she's right that it could just be the stress of coming back here, but I still feel like there is something more going on with them. Based on the available information, however, her theory is much more solid and I cling to it. Something in my gut, something deep inside, tells me there is more to this story, more information we are missing. Unfortunately, I don't know how to put that into words, and the last thing I want to do is waste her time with paranoid theories. "What would you do in my shoes Ruby?"

Chuckling, she says, "You don't get to be my age by making a lot of guesses Jackson. You try to figure things out, but you know there is always a chance you're wrong if you want to be smart. If I were you, I would do what you're already doing. Try to figure it out, try to learn about the town, and be ready in case they need you. It might be something, but it might be nothing, and in my experience, you won't know until it's too late to plan." She must be able to tell I was hoping for some magic or wisdom. She pats my shoulder, and shrugs with an exaggerated smile that makes me giggle.

We sit out on the porch for a few more hours. More than once, her granddaughter comes out to check on her and refill her tea. They have been living together for years now, and she finds it hilarious that, "I raised my baby girl here and she couldn't wait to get out of this place, but then she raised her girl in Atlanta and watched her run here as fast as she could." I find it funny too. While her daughter went into the law following Ruby's activist streak, her granddaughter got the artistic desire, and makes her living creating prints, jewelry, and paintings she sells through her own online store and at Sylus and Lacey's shops in town. At one point, we invite her to stay and chat, but she declines, and Ruby explains that, "Lessie just don't like people all that much, so don't take no offense. Ever since she was little, she preferred to spend her time alone with her art. She'll talk to you when she's ready, and she's seen more of you." I smile thinking I know exactly how she feels since I feel that way a lot of the time too.

As the sun falls from the sky, I begin getting ready to leave, and she thanks me for coming by and invites me to come back anytime. "Maybe sometimes you'll bring me some of that pie from Chuck's," she says and I agree to do so. In fact, I swing back by the next day just to say hello, drop off autographed copies of each of my books for her daughter as well as a copy of the unpublished story, and bring enough pie for her, Lessie, and the great grandkids to hopefully have their fill. She points up at the sky, and I look in the same direction to see beautiful purple and orange tinges shaping the horizon. We both stand there smiling. I'm halfway down the porch steps when I realize I forgot something I wanted to ask her.

"Hey Ruby, do you know why it's called Queens?"

She walks to the edge of the porch just above where I am standing, and says, "Oh my, I think you'll like this one." She chuckles, and asks, "So you know about the whorehouse that was here before it was town? Did you get that in your research?" I nod, and she continues, "Well, a lot of people here in town don't like it, but this place was founded – as a town at least – by some freed black people who owned farms in the area. My little girl, she likes family tree type stuff, thinks we might even be related to one of the families. I would like that. Anyway, even at the best points of reconstruction, though, they still

111

needed the white families' cooperation to get things done, you see. Well, ole Mr. Rams, the leader of the farmers wanting to make this an official town, you see, he went out to see the fella that ran the big farm where the whorehouse was. You see, if he got that guy on board, then the other white families, all of them had much less than that guy, would come along with the idea for a town."

She walks back over to the swing, takes another sip of her latest sweet tea, and comes back to the edge of the porch. "Okay, so, he went out to see that fella, and the fella was interested in a town, but only if he could name it. He apparently had started that there whorehouse not only because his farm was having trouble, no sir, he had also been in love with a freed black woman who left with her family when they headed north in search of better jobs. He was so heartbroken, and his wife who found out was so angry and rumor was she even tried to kill him once but I don't know if that's true, that he ended up all alone on that farm with his workers who he paid without too much hassle, which was something at the time, you see. So," she says and starts chuckling again and takes a little break to catch her breath, "Excuse me, ooh, that's the cost of a good day of talking right there."

She took another swig of her tea and continued, "So, you see, the whorehouse became his only real social life and family. He hired the girls and helped them out, and gave them a place to stay, and remember poor girls of a lot of colors had almost nothing at the time. So, when Mr. Rams came to see him, well, he said he would support the town idea, and even rally support for it from his customers. That basically meant most of the white men in town and at that time, it also meant most of the people who could have a say in town. You see, he just wanted to name the town, and he wanted to name it after the love of his life, that little black girl who moved north. As it turns out, her name – at least the one she used with him – was Queens so that became the name of the town, but the story got lost over the years, my mama said, because white people didn't like the thought of living in a town named by a whorehouse owner to honor a black woman he loved."

She lets out a long, loud laugh and smacks the railing on the porch. "It's kind of funny because when I was a little girl everyone, or at least everyone in the black part of town, knew this story, but now it seems like all people remember is that there was once a whorehouse here." She laughs some more, and continues, "My husband used to say it says a lot about a place what they remember and what they forget, and I've always thought the name of this town is a perfect example of that."

With the name of the town finally explained, we said goodnight in between our respective chuckles, and I headed back down to the sidewalk where the bike I found in Chuck's garage had been sitting for hours. I waved to Ruby as I got on the bike, and made my way down Main Street toward our house. The whole way, I had this image in my head of the heartbroken whorehouse owner negotiating with Mr. Rams in hopes of honoring the original queen of this place. I also thought about the fact that I just spent an entire day with someone half a century older than me who had more passion and energy than damn near anyone I ever met. In the end, I arrived at the house wondering if maybe Ruby was right, and there was nothing to worry about with Crystal and Lee. I didn't think so, but I hoped I was wrong this time.

CHAPTER 17

The sun shone through my windshield as I pulled into the parking lot at "Matt's flea market – Open every Saturdays and Sunday – Bring the Family" one Sunday morning three months after meeting Ruby. I was finally starting to get used to living in Queens, and it felt like Queens was used to me. I still faced a daily barrage of dirty looks, and it was obvious that many people were not happy to see me. At the same time, I developed my own network of friends that eased the feelings of 'go home' I still got from much of the town's folk.

The night before, I was having dinner with Sylus and his family when I mentioned that I wished there was a good place to get CDs in the area. As much as I love my digital and vinyl collections, sometimes I just like the feeling of sliding a CD into the player in my car, and driving while it unwinds its story of songs. Lacey managed to cover all my vinyl needs, and digital media was easy to get online, but I wanted a local option – or even semi-local – for CDs.

"Have you tried Matt's," Sylus asked while refilling his wife Rhonda's wine glass.

"Matt's?"

"Yeah, the flea market that's open every Saturdays," Rhonda said with a smile.

"Nope, I haven't made it out there yet."

"There is this old white guy out there, Jimmy I think his name is, that sells CDs for cheap and in pretty good condition. You should try that out, and see what he's got," Sylus said sitting back down at the table. Dinner was long over, but at this house, dinner was more of an excuse to stay up late chatting about music, art, and gossip. Rhonda worked at the military base on the outskirts of Augusta, and rarely wanted to go out after the long commute each day. Years earlier, they started having these dinners with selected friends to be social and not add more time to her already long days.

"You'll probably like it," Rhonda says, "He actually has a pretty diverse selection most weekends and most things are only about a buck or two. Sylus is always too busy looking at movies and old crap to pay any attention." Sylus nods in a way that says she is correct, and we all share a laugh before moving on to talk about an art show coming to Louisville. An artist who does wood cuts and works at the university in Augusta is doing a show, and all of us are planning to go out to the opening together. We also want to see the "one girl in the world at least so far" that made Lacey question her sexuality when she took classes with the artist in college, and provide Lacey with support for the reunion.

When I arrived at the flea market, the place was jumping and full of more people than I thought lived in the whole area. It was arranged in five rows wherein the odd rows were each covered buildings and the other even rows were covered but more open to the elements. Out front, there was also a farmer's mart with no covering composed of the same tables I noticed on my way into town. As I entered the parking lot, I decided the left side of the structure looked best, and parked in one of the dirt spaces on that side, but near the back so I could enter at the beginning of a row. Apparently, the people who designed the place – maybe Matt, I thought – had similar plans because I entered at the bottom of Row One.

I always loved flea markets and other outdoor shopping settings, and had been looking forward to checking the place out since I arrived in town. Like Rhonda, I still got a little bit of a kick out of the sign, and I still wondered if it was somehow intentional or just a typo that never got corrected. I entered from the back of the building, and found myself walking past the types of booths that seem to populate flea markets all over the southeast. There were DVDs, comic books, Precious Moments figurines, stuffed animals, children's toys, and flags sitting beside shops specializing in vaporizers, airbrush services, novelty license plates, and rummage sales from people's garages. There was, in the middle of row three, the obligatory rug shop, appliance store, and food court. There were places to buy gun racks, books, baby clothes, and hundreds of different dollar items. Finally, and necessary Marcus would say when we went with Lee out to the flea market in Pinellas Park, Florida, there were so many video games, like they were everywhere and all different types, years, and makes.

I walked through the rows watching the people, and checking out a few things here and there. I rarely spent any money on anything other than books and music, but I enjoyed looking around. You never knew what awaited you at a flea market, and for me, that was a big part of the fun. I walked past a group of white teenagers demonstrating some stun guns they were selling, and a guy with an accent that reminded me of my days in Texas selling hand crafted, souvenir beer steins. I listened to children playing, crying, and sometimes doing both at once. I watched tired adults chase them around the rows, and wondered why anyone would ever volunteer for such a thing. I even stopped by the "What does the Bible really say" booth that seems to be at every flea market. It was a nice way to spend a Sunday afternoon.

I finally found myself on row five where the guy my friends thought was called Jimmy had three booths full of CDs in boxes and tables in front of each one with vinyl albums that did not look like they were in the best condition. I agreed with Rhonda about the selection. There were CD reissues of old 60's and 70's soul records alongside Industrial Metal, mainstream Country releases, and even a collection of Power Metal. The guy even had obscure things like Lounge music, Electro pop, and 1980's indie rock. I was looking through a collection of Americana albums in a box marked one dollar when I found a couple Lucinda Williams releases I wanted. I grabbed them both, and moved on to a couple boxes of Classic Rock and Soul. I didn't find anything in those boxes so I kept moving.

I was looking at a set of punk albums including an Against Me album I didn't have on CD yet as I thought about my conversation with May the previous day. She already read the books I got her in Milledgeville, and wanted to know more about the two on Transgender History. She told me that she never felt comfortable in her body, and thought she would be happier as a boy a few weeks before at the diner. Now, however, she was looking for concrete examples of other people who felt the same way, and the ways people went about making that change. I decided to pick up an extra Against Me album to give to her with the pamphlets, articles, and contact information for a friend in Florida that I was already planning to share next time I saw her. I spent an hour with my friend on the phone yesterday afternoon

117

figuring out both the options for her if she wanted to transition, and options for school and employment down there. He was confident that he could help, and agreed to give her his email address and share his own history of transitioning in his twenties. I was just hoping the information would help her do what was best for her life.

After paying Jimmy for my CDs and smiling about how little they seemed to cost these days, I continued down row five where the bookstore was located. I wondered if someone with my own tastes had come up with the idea of having row five basically be a long tunnel of books and music only. I was chuckling about this, and feeling quite good until I found a copy of my first novel for fifty cents. Ouch, I thought at first, but then I wondered if it might be fun to buy the thing and leave it on the doorstep of the bookstore in town for Jenny to find. Although I was sure it would be fun, I didn't feel like going downtown so I decided to shelve the idea for a later date.

I was almost all the way through the racks of books that took up four stalls when I found Samantha studying a John Irving novel. I said hello to her, and she almost jumped out of her skin. Slowly, she said, ever so softly, "Hello."

"Are you finding anything good?"

Nodding vigorously and showing more emotion than I thought the kid was capable of at that point, she said or whispered really, "Oh yeah, but the problem is I can only afford to get one at a time so I have to pick which one." She blushes and gestures to a basket full of books. I remembered Ruby and Kate saying they looked out for the kid, who might have been one of the smartest people in the state, because the kid's mom was struggling to get by after getting out of an abusive marriage over in Waynesboro a couple years before. I also knew the kid was best friends with May, and aside from me, May's main outlet in town.

"Can I take a look," I ask, and she nods blushing again.

I look through the basket where she has twelve novels neatly organized. There are a couple fantasy books from the *Wheel of Time* series, a collection of poems by Elizabeth Bishop, and a few general fiction books by the likes of Flannery O'Connor and Alice Walker. She has a copy of my favorite Stephen King book – *Lisey's Story* – with a worn-out cover. I do the math in my head, and with the Irving novel she is holding and the Helen Fielding novel she just picked up from the shelf, we're only talking about 20 bucks. Thinking about the cost, I feel myself transported to another time and place.

I was in high school when I realized how much I loved reading. I had a teacher who took an interest in me, Mrs. Morgan, and let me go to the library during classes since I couldn't stay after school or come early. I would check out all five books we were allowed at the time, and read them in a few days. I kept doing this until I basically exhausted the supply in our school library. I've since seen bathrooms bigger than that library. When the library stopped working for me, I started going to a local bookshop where the owner would let kids just sit around and read if we bought books occasionally and told others about the shop. I remember wishing for a day where I could afford to have books whenever I wanted them, and as I stood there in the flea market looking at Samantha's basket, I realized I accomplished that dream without even noticing.

"Does your mom mind you having all these books," I asked because I had already learned that books were not always considered good in southern cities and towns. I also knew from Ruby and Kate that her mom was a good parent doing her best with few resources, and I didn't want to cause any extra problems for her.

"Nope, she says if she ever gets rich she's going to get me a whole library, and she makes sure I always get at least enough money in the budget for a book a week."

"Because I think you should get them all, the whole basket and those two in your hands."

"I've only got two dollars this week, well, I have three but mom says never use all you have just in case you need it later."

"That doesn't matter, I have money. I will get them for you if you want them." I was channeling my inner Crystal and Lee. Crystal would randomly hand out money to people who asked for change on the streets, sometimes giving them all the cash she had. At one point, she only carried cash to give it away to people. It was her way of giving back, aside from the charities our family donated to each year, after making it. Lee, in a similar fashion, often devoted his cooking talents and sports connections to providing food and recreation for homeless and poor youth when we were in Tampa. He would spend whole weekends feeding and playing with people who didn't have as much as we did. I always admired the two of them for these things, and I started looking for chances to do the same when I could.

"Really," she says, and she looks like she's going to cry.

"If you want and you promise your mom won't be mad."

"Yes, yes yes, and my mom will love it." She is correct. Her mother calls me that night to say thanks multiple times even as I try to say no thanks is necessary. After I get off the phone, I also learn from Crystal that we don't charge Samantha or her mom when they eat at Chuck's and that her and Lee adopted the same policy for some of the other people struggling in town. I begin to wonder what are some other things I – or we – might do to help people in the town that are struggling in this economy, and smile as I watch Samantha practically skip out of the row in search of her mother and in anticipation of her new stack of books.

For a moment, I just stand there remembering Ruby's description of the charitable drives the churches are doing, and Lacey's volunteer work at the school. I think about the trailer parks in town, the couple stores here and there that are empty or going out of business since I've gotten to town. I think about the news coverage celebrating the economic recovery, and the high spirits with new developments and job programs on the news while I was in Tampa. I look around me, and wonder, will any of these good things make their way out here to small towns like Queens isolated from the cities, removed from the polling and survey research centers of the nation, and built upon the factory and other manual labor that seems to increasingly disappear from our nation. At that moment, I wonder just how many policy experts, political candidates, or researchers have ever spent time talking to people at a flea market, and what the scientific facts or media coverage might look like if they did.

As is often the case in flea markets I have visited, there is a center row in Matt's that stretches the width of the market and provides easy access to the other rows. It holds coffee carts, a place selling beer, and a few other shops. Having finished with my own needs, I decide to take this path out of the place. Walking through the center aisle, I find myself again enjoying the sights, chaos, and noise of strangers killing time on the weekend. As I turn onto row one, however, I notice something I didn't see the first time through the structure. Later, I will think about the ways little decisions – like a few extra minutes in a flea market created by a random observation – combine to influence the course of people's lives.

The comic stand has a book on display that has Alice Cooper's name on the cover. I didn't know there were Alice Cooper comics, I think, but Crys would love that. It turns out the book is a hybrid comic novel based on *The Last Temptation*. Knowing how much Crystal loves that record, I grab the book and go inside the shop. The comic merchant explains that the comics were made as a continuation of the story, and the artwork was approved by Cooper. I buy the book, and begin looking forward to Crystal's reaction.

At the same time, I decide to go into the DVD shop at the entrance where I came in earlier, and see if I can find Lee a copy of the silly *Space Jam* movie he loves since his copy finally broke the week before after it's fifteenth million play. I honestly was hoping to never see the film again, but love makes us do crazy things. To my surprise, they have a copy of it, on Blu-Ray in fact, and I grab it and start thinking this must be my lucky day. This thought runs through my head as I step out of the shop, turn towards where my car is parked, and find myself face to face with "my favorite."

CHAPTER 18

Our eyes meet and he looks about as shocked as I am. It's been more than a year since we saw each other, and months since I received and ignored his last text message. He looks just as good as ever, but I'm having trouble processing anything beyond an overwhelming sense of shock. "Excuse me," he says with a bit of a stutter and the sound of fear coloring his voice. I say the same, and he walks past me into the flea market. I stare after him for a few seconds, and he looks back at me twice. What is he doing in Queens? How is this even possible? I stand there for a few minutes, probably looking like an idiot who has gotten lost or something equally unflattering, but all that happens is the same question keeps running through my head on a loop – what the hell is he doing *here*?

I consider going after him, but decide against it. I'm a little overwhelmed, and I don't know if this is good, bad, or something else. On the one hand, he has been a lot of fun over the past decade, and especially with both my spouses seeming more and more distant of late, it might be nice to revisit him. On the other hand, we're a long way from Tampa and the anonymity that made our times together so much fun for both of us, and the only answer I can come up with to the question running through my head is that he lives somewhere around here. I don't remember anyone around town mentioning the name Paul, but I also never believed that was necessarily his real name. Hell, to him, I'm a marketing specialist – whatever that means – named Marshall. I lifted my own name and limited bio off a childhood friend's Facebook profile, and I wouldn't be surprised if he did a similar thing since the whole point was to step outside of our daily lives.

As I reached my car, I thought about the first time I saw my favorite, or Paul, or whatever his real name was, sitting alone at a bar and restaurant in Ybor City. Since I spent most of my time in South Tampa, St. Pete, and up in the northern part of the city near USF when I was out with my family, Ybor became my favorite place to, as one old guy that hung out, or lived I wasn't sure, at the Liquid Bar put it, "cruise for new friends." I would go to Liquid, New World Brewery or one of the other bars, and spend the night dancing and drinking. Occasionally, these escapades led to more, but most of the time the flirting and petting was more than enough to meet my extra-marital needs. Afterwards, I would always swing by the Bricks to sober up before driving and to get an espresso since they were open late and had damn good coffee. I would sit outside, in the back on the little deck or in the front on the sidewalk, and think about the night before going home to Lee and Crystal.

I was sitting out back one of these nights when he came outside looking nervous, a little scared, and honestly a bit overwhelmed. I recognized that look after years of hanging out in such neighborhoods, he was new or visiting in hopes of finding something missing in his life. Since such spaces were so useful to my younger self, I always responded to that look by seeking to make the person comfortable. I offered him a seat, and over the next hour I learned that he worked in education (maybe), was from upstate (maybe), was on vacation (likely true), but was new to the whole "you know, this, thing" (probably true). He was obviously still working through issues many of us – if not all – do in this society, but he was cute and his issues were not my concern. We had a nice chat and I gave him my burner-phone number when I left.

I was very serious about boundaries between personal and casual relationships. I think about that burner phone – comfortably resting in my den at Chuck's / our house at present – I used in such moments, and made sure that number was never associated with my real life. I learned this trick from a closeted gay man named Ty in Miami who had been navigating multiple lives for over two decades when we first hooked up. I was sure Paul was taking similar countermeasures because his clothes, demeanor, and mannerisms did not suggest someone who could only afford a pre-paid Tracfone. The wonderful thing I learned about cities over the years was people rarely ventured outside their established patterns, neighborhoods, and commutes. As a result, it was easy to hide in plain sight in any given neighborhood if one avoided that neighborhood the rest of the time.

I was thinking about these tactics and wondering how people might pull off similar dual lives in small towns as I drove out of the parking lot that day. One way, I figured, was to only live one part of their lives when they were on vacation. If Paul lived here, I was thinking maybe that was the approach he had come up with. I remember occasionally wondering where he was and how he lived, but I never bothered to try to find out because I didn't want my own anonymity unraveled. I remember Lee finding it hilarious that the guy's name could be a Biblical admonition against what we were doing, and Crystal quoting part of Paul's letter to the Romans one night when I was leaving to see Paul. We had more fun with that gag over the years than was likely warranted. I remember the night an acquaintance saw us out on the town, and called me by my actual name leading me to tell Paul that was just a fake name I gave some people I met in bars. I remember this didn't seem to faze him at all.

I also remember being surprised the day after we met to get a text from Paul. We spent the week talking, kissing, and grabbing dinners in Ybor. Nothing else happened on that trip, and I wrote it off as a fun fling when he left town until he texted me about a year later. On that trip, we became sexually active – something I cleared with Lee and Crys during the previous trip – and spent three weeks hanging out in his hotel room and my – maybe ours who knew – city. He reminded me of Lee with his constant musings about heaven and hell. He reminded me of Crys with his smartass humor and clipped responses to anything potentially emotional or hinting at the past. He also reminded me of Kid back in Atlanta because there was always something somber hiding just behind his smile. I didn't know, and didn't want to know, where that melancholy came from, but I couldn't avoid noticing it each year.

He seemed especially down whenever he talked about Tampa. He said he initially decided to come to the city because an old love lived here once, and seemed to enjoy it. He wanted to see what it was like, and after a bit of studying, he learned about Ybor City and became even more curious. He said he only expected to come one time to check it out, but then we met and something about me reminded him of a close friend from when he was younger. Whenever he talked about these things, I would find myself looking at the, to my eyes, obvious indention on his ring finger that suggested he had a life with someone else somewhere. I remember wondering if he wound up in my arms each year because of something missing in that life and an inability to leave it behind just the same.

For a minute after seeing him, I fell into the classic trap wherein one sees their own place of residence as the only one. This led me to wonder if he lived in Queens, but as I drove down Queens Boulevard, it hit me that there wasn't another flea market – except for a tiny antique mart between here and Milledgeville – in this area. The closest one was over on the south side of Augusta, and one thing I was sure I knew about Paul or my favorite was that he collected antiques. He could easily live in Louisville, Waynesboro, Wrens or any of the other small towns around here. He could live in Augusta, and just be out on the weekend looking for antiques in the country. He could even live over in South Carolina on the other side of Augusta in one of the small towns like the one Lacey came from. There was no guarantee that I would ever see him again, or that he would ever show up in Queens.

This thought comforted me a little as I pulled into the gas station near our neighborhood to purchase a pack of cigarettes that I wasn't supposed to have but felt like I needed. While he might live elsewhere, it was also possible that he was one of the many people in this town I had not yet met. If so, I thought as I stood out in the parking lot of the gas station smoking a cigarette, he could walk into Chuck's any day now, he could show up at our house when the cable or Internet or water went out, or we could have meetings like the one at the flea market anywhere in town at any time. I didn't like this idea for two reasons. First, I was never all that comfortable with surprises in the first place, and I didn't like the thought of walking around town always on guard for the next awkward moment. Second, I was basically famous or infamous in town, which meant he might very well know who I was even though I had no clue who he was, and that felt strange to me.

I lit a second cigarette I wasn't supposed to have thinking about the last time we saw each other, back when things were so simple, back when my spouses didn't feel like strangers passing in the night, back before that damned Chuck had to fuck with things by dying. We spent the day in his room at the Marriott downtown, and we were having a late dinner at the Acropolis Greek restaurant on 7th Avenue. He was halfway through his gyro plate, and I was enjoying a splendid Greek salad – the same thing I got when Lee, Crystal and I went to the Acropolis over in St. Pete some weekends after looking at records or catching a show at the State Theatre. Lee was at home packing everything up for a trip we were taking to Miami the following week, and Crystal was at a dinner party Alice was hosting for a visiting lesbian poet over in St. Pete. At the time, it was just another night out on the town.

In hindsight, however, that night reminds me of all that has changed since. At the time, Crys, Lee, and I were in sync – even when any of us were fighting – but we don't feel that way anymore. At the time, we didn't know Chuck would die. At the time, I held a disdain for small towns that I'm slowly realizing was not fair or all that realistic in the first place. The places are just as good, bad, and everywhere in between as any city I have lived in during my life. At the time, Lee was on the fast track with his reporting career, and Crystal was celebrating the latest in a long row of honors in her profession. Now, Lee runs a grill and Crystal manages the books for the grill. At the time, Paul was my favorite hobby that emerged like clockwork each year to release some stress, and I never thought I would ever want or need to know much about him.

Our time was carefree energy in a careful world. It was evenings in hotel rooms, at local restaurants, and in clubs and bars where we were each relatively unknown to anyone who mattered in our daily lives. It was late night strolls, drinking too much, and stolen kisses on corners and in parking garages. It was fun. It was easy. It was only ever for a little while, and only confined to the limited time we saw each other every year. We were teenagers again. We were living in the moment for just a few days before schedules and requirements came back to life. We were on vacation, and would at some point just go home with no concerns about the other. Now, we were meeting accidentally in a place where people like us were, at best, tolerated amidst a barrage of questions, and at worse, in danger.

I was also aware that I somehow changed a lot in the time since that night. I was no longer afraid of small towns, but I still thought the city would always be a better fit for me. I was no longer as secure in my marriage now that each of my spouses seemed to be hiding something or struggling with something I could not access. I was no longer completely isolated since everyone in town seemed to know who I was, and little May had basically adopted me as her guide to what or who she wanted to be. I no longer thought of Chuck as a random figure somewhere in Crys and Lee's past life, but rather saw him as the evil source of all this change. Most surprising to me as I finished the sixth smoke I wasn't supposed to have in that gas station parking lot, I was no longer comfortable knowing nothing about my favorite, Paul, or whatever his name was. At that moment, I needed to know who he was if for no other reason than to avoid the shock and worry I felt when he materialized at the flea market that day.

CHAPTER 19

As much as I wanted to figure out who Paul might be, I had to put this goal out of my mind when I got home that day. As I pulled up in our backyard, I saw May sitting on the steps of our porch, and it looked like she had been crying. I took a deep breath, put aside my concerns about Paul or whatever his name might be, and got out of the car. As I walked up to the porch, I said hello and asked her what was going on and why she looked so sad. She wiped her face, raised her head to show those always penetrating blue eyes, and sighed in a way that reminded me of Crys in tough moments over the years or Lee when he was trying to figure something out.

"I think I'm a boy."

"Okay, what do you mean by that," I said taking a seat beside her on the back steps of the deck, and pulling out a cigarette from the pack I wasn't supposed to have. My mind immediately summoned my time with River, all the advice I got from him about how to be supportive in this situation, all the negative shit he had to deal with as he wrestled with this exact experience, and all the ways I could help now with my current resources that I could only dream of back then. I took a deep breath ready for whatever May might say, and heard River in my head telling a trans-woman at the time, "I'll be the rock for you that I never had."

"I've been reading all those books, and I keep feeling like I'm reading about me with the trans ones. I've always felt like my body was more like a, I don't know, a cage maybe, or something like that, than, like, a body. I was a tomboy, as my mom called it, but then when I got older I had to behave, I don't know, she would say 'like a lady.' I never liked that because I didn't want to be a lady. I don't know, I hid it, like, the boy stuff I kept doing and liking, like, I pretended to behave like my mom wanted, but I didn't like it. So, like I told you before, I would wear baggy clothes because I didn't like how I looked, like, my body just felt wrong the older I got. I don't know how to say it really."

I remembered our first meeting, and the way May appeared in comparison to her – no their for now and maybe he later, I thought, stop gendering her, I mean them, Jackson – sisters. I thought about how curious and awkward they were with the LGBT fiction and non-fiction, and how nervous they were talking about it and asking questions. May was not nervous at all now. Today, May sounded more certain, composed, and vocal than I would have thought possible when we first met. I remembered the first time I came across positive notions of bisexuality and polyamory, and I could see the same look in May's eyes.

My second novel – the one that May said was their favorite from the start – contained a character, based on a guy named Nick in Orlando that Lee developed a massive crush on years ago, who transitioned from female-to-male. The character also had elements of River's personality, and experiences we shared – good and bad – in college as he transitioned. Sadly for Lee, Nick was monogamous, and had been with an amazing woman named Taylor for over a decade at that point. Sadly for me, River was far too mature and self-assured for the younger me to keep up with in the long run. As I sat there with May, I wondered if they saw themselves in these people and the character based on them, and if that drew May to me in the first place rather than my relationship. I remembered, though I felt bad for not noticing it in the moment, that May looked disappointed when they learned I was not transgender myself, but seemed relieved to learn I dated transgender people. I sat there thinking about just how much courage this kid had to have to open this conversation in a small town in Georgia.

"So, this is why you were so curious about transition resources and materials?"

"Yeah, I was reading the history book, I felt like it was about me, I don't know, maybe that sounds crazy."

"No, it doesn't, I felt the same way when I first found materials about bi people. I felt like a whole new world of people just like me opened up out of nowhere, and I wanted to know every part of it. It was the same thing River went through with trans books and I went through again later learning about poly people. Lee and Crys can relate too."

"That's exactly how I feel right now. So, what do I do?"

"Well, no one can tell you that May. Do you think you can talk about this with your parents or with your sisters?"

"I don't think so. My mom is really against this kind of stuff, and I saw the way her and her friends treated the lesbian couple that used to live in town. My sisters, I don't know, I think April might know because she's seen me trying on dad's clothes and stuff, but she hasn't said anything. June is more like my mom and I don't think she would keep it secret from my mom because they talk about everything."

"Okay, well, you have me, and with your permission I could tell Crys and Lee, and they would be there for you, but only if that's okay with you. Do you have anyone else?" I feel myself quoting River and other people who accepted me when I was younger.

"My friend Samantha kind of suggested it a couple years ago after she read your novel, and I think she would be cool with it. Miss Kate, over at the library, has always been nice to me, and helped me find things online before you moved here, and Miss Laccy at the record store is the only one who knows how I feel. She's the one who told me to talk to you. She also told me you thought I was a boy at first, like you saw me, I guess, and that felt good if that makes any sense. I also think Miss Ruby would be nice about it, she's always taught us everyone has to be true to themselves and she had a friend like me she mentioned in a story she was telling us one day."

"That's good. So, you've got a little network of support, and that's important. You just turned eighteen recently, so you're an adult and your parents can't commit you or anything like that. You're also done with high school now, so you won't have to stay here if you don't want to, and we're working on getting you to a good college already. Crys can help a lot with that too, especially if she knows why you might want to get out of here. I guess that means you just have to figure out what you want, and decide if you want to do that here or somewhere else."

"Speaking of my parents, they say the people on television, like the bathroom stuff, are sick. Is it possible that they're right and I'm just sick?"

I hear the fear in May's voice, and turn their face to mine so we are eye to eye as I say, "No, there is nothing sick about you May. Crystal has even done some of this research, and the fact is that people like you – hell even people like me – have existed throughout recorded human history and even been celebrated in many cases. There is nothing wrong with you. The people who say bad things about trans people are the sick ones, they have been misled by hate and fear and often religion to believe things that are not true."

"I just really worry about it sometimes, but that's what Miss Lacey says, she says I'm normal, but the world is full of people who don't like anything different from them."

"She is right," I say and think about how many times Crystal, Lee, and I have had similar conversations with LGBT students who come to the bi professor in search of answers. All that pain and fear created by people who see something different from them and decide on the spot that it must be bad simply because they cannot understand it. Their own opinion seems obvious to them, and they guard that opinion by attacking anything different. "I'm sorry you even have to feel those things, and that we – your elders – have not yet done better combatting that stuff. It's the same stuff Lee, Crystal, me, and everyone else like us heard growing up, and just like for us, it is terrible for you to have to hear, but also completely false."

"I just don't know what to do, but I do know how I feel."

"I remember that tough spot very clearly myself May."

"I got into that first program your friend recommended me for in Tampa a couple months back. So, it looks like I am going to college, that part is already set up thanks to y'all, and they said there are groups for people like me there."

"Great! There are people who will support you there, and there are resources through the school too that might be helpful for you. Congratulations college kid!"

"I don't think my family will like me going so far away, but I think it might be best for me. Miss Kate has a friend in Orlando that works with women's health groups, and she said she could probably help me get an internship or maybe even a part time job during the school year. But, I'm still going to have to find loans or something if my family won't help me."

"Don't worry about that right now. You worry about figuring out what you want to do, and if you need help financially, our little family can help you out, and Crystal might hurt us if she finds out your situation and we don't jump to help you."

They laugh for the first time that day, "If anyone knows about wanting out of here, I guess it's her right."

"Yep, and combine that with her obsession with justice, and you got a perfect storm."

"It's okay if you tell them about me."

"Are you sure?"

"Yes, I trust y'all, and you're the whole reason I even have the chance to go south for a career and maybe a real life."

"No, I'm not May. You did the work, in school and talking with the people I connected you to, not me. You are the whole reason you have a chance to follow your dreams, I just helped. You're the brave one in this story, don't forget that."

Blushing, May says, "I guess so," and we just sit there for a little while talking about Florida, talking about transition options and resources, and talking about the town. I haven't met May's parents that I know of, but I'm a worried about them if they were part of the crew that convinced that other couple to leave town. I find myself thinking about just how much difference a couple phone calls, like the ones I made on May's behalf, can make in someone's life. I find myself feeling even more admiration for Lacey and Kate – whose best friend in college, as she told me, was a non-binary trans person and she probably suspected where May's questions were coming from – for providing safe spaces for May. I wonder how much of an effect we could have on the ways trans kids experience the world if all of them had safe spaces to be or figure out themselves.

Later in the evening, May finally gets ready to go home again. I give them all the materials I found on transition, the books I picked up on my latest Amazon hunt, and the Against Me CD I picked up at the flea market. "The lead singer of the band is really trans," May asks.

"Yes, she is, and writes and sings about it on this CD."

"That is so cool," May says turning the CD case over in their hands and wearing the biggest smile I've ever seen on their face. "She must be really brave."

"I would have to agree," I say smiling at them and taking their hand, "And so are you no matter what you decide you want your life to be. It takes a lot of courage to be true to yourself in this world and you should be proud of yourself for doing that."

May nods and heads off into the night. I take a seat on the back porch, and light another cigarette I am not supposed to have. I sit there watching the sky, thinking about Paul or whatever his name is, and thinking about May. Before having the second cigarette I'm not supposed to have in the same spot, I go inside and grab a drink. As I sit there, drink in one hand, cigarette in the other, about an hour after May leaves, my spouses arrive home together laughing and holding hands for the first time in what seems like an eternity. They are talking about some funny dance Shelby was doing in the restaurant and giggling when they spot me. Both accelerate their pace, and I find myself in a group hug simultaneously loving the moment and realizing how rare these have become.

"How was your day babe," Lee asks as Crystal lights one of the smokes I'm not supposed to have.

"Interesting," I say, and then fill them in on May's latest news. I tell them about May's thoughts on their own gender, acceptance at USF and into our friend's Public Health cluster program, and anticipated family reaction if they find out.

"That must be so hard for May," Crystal says when I finish, "And I hope you told them that they can reach out to us at any time, and that we'll help however we can."

"I did."

"So do we call May 'he' now or do we do the gender neutral thing like with Crys' research assistant last semester, or do we just keep things the same until we know more," Lee says smiling at the fact that he's gotten much better at this stuff since his crush on Nick. Before then, Lee was utterly confused by all the, as he used to say, "gender stuff." Though it took some practice, the last few years we watched him experience a complete transformation from 'well they should be equal though I don't get it' to 'how can people not understand this stuff, they're just like us and need the same support and respect as anyone else damn it.' We have even seen Lee correct someone's mis-gendering of other people, and both of us, in that moment, were amazed when he told us, "I'm so ashamed that I used to do that shit, what was wrong with me."

"For right now, we just keep quiet and be there for May. I'm using gender neutral language, but May has not requested anything specific. May said they like the gender neutral language right now, but they will let me know when or if that changes. Right now, they are figuring out who they are, what they want, and what they will do, so we just be there for them."

"Sounds good to me," they both say at the same time, and we all laugh. Lee continues, "I'm still friendly with that doctor in Miami, remember the straight guy whose daughter came out as trans right after we moved to Tampa, if May needs another professional to talk to who won't act like a jerk. I'm also still in touch with Jamie if May needs to talk to someone who did transition socially and medically, and Jamie's fiancé is non-binary if that helps too. We could also reach out to Nick and Taylor still works with that LGBT youth group in Orlando."

"I also have a good working relationship with the resource center on campus, and we can tap into that for May when they move down. It took some time, but the sexuality group also has a trans and bi component on campus too, and that might also be good for May."

"I love you both so much right now," I say and they both giggle and smile at me. We sit out on the porch most of the night just talking and being together again. I don't know what happened to the distance that seemed to live between them since I got to town, but for that night, it was gone and we were us again. We laughed, we told old stories and new ones, and Lee even did a pretty good – according to Crys – imitation of the dance Shelby was doing in Chuck's to the delight of all the customers. Crys didn't take a walk that night for the first time since I got to town, and Lee didn't mention or study religion either. Instead, later in the evening the three of us finally went to the same bedroom for the first time in Queens.

CHAPTER 20

I have read that in every long-term relationship there are roles that the partners play beyond the aspects of their day to day lives. Sometimes these roles are there from the start, and sometimes they develop over time. In our family, the roles were clear early on, and never really changed. Lee, from as far back as I could remember, had always been the peacemaker and the source of conflict resolution. Whether the dispute was big or small, short or long term, personal or professional, Lee would always – even if it took some time – find a way to bring us all back together in some form of compromise.

Crystal had always been the brain. Anything that required planning, managing, balancing, adjusting, or just plain forethought also involved Lee and I deferring to Crystal's advice. She was just plain smarter than us, and we both loved and hated this fact at different times. If our family needed to make sense of something or figure out how to accomplish something, we all ran to Crys for help. This was also a large part of the reason we always followed her career wherever it took us. On some level, we all knew that Crys was our leader, and Lee and I did better when we followed her commands. No matter the situation, Crystal would figure it out in nine or more ways, and then direct our family's operation.

I had a role in our family as well, but it was of a different sort. By any measure or conceptualization, to use Crys' wording, I was the screw up. If something was going to go wrong, odds were good I would be the source. When the porch almost fell apart at our place in Miami, it was due to a chemistry experiment I did for a still never written novel that messed up the wood some way I still don't understand. Each time our mortgage payment did not get mailed quite on time, it was my turn to handle it. When Crystal missed a big impromptu pre-tenure meeting with the faculty of her department while they faced an unforeseen crisis, it was because I was the one who answered the phone and forgot to write down the message. When Lee got the big fat ticket for driving without insurance, it was because I had forgotten to handle the insurance payment. No matter the situation, if something was going to go wrong without warning, I was likely responsible in some way.

Being the kind and loving people they are, my spouses tried to spin this in a favorable way even though it drove them crazy. Crystal would say I was the agent of chaos that kept us all from getting boring. Lee would say I was our constant reminder of the impetuousness and thrill of youth. I would say I just was not very good at being an adult, and I had the data to back the assertion up. I did not have the familial, financial, communal, professional, or even long-term relationship credentials they had. I spent most of my life alone bouncing from place to place simply trying to survive and have fun before I met them. No one ever taught me about bills, savings, contracts, intimacy, responsibility, or any of the other stuff they already knew quite well. River tried for longer than anyone else, but I was likely even more un-trainable before I lost him. Something about that pain grew me up at least enough for Crystal and Lee to teach me a few things. Of course, I never fully became much of an adult. As Deidre liked to say, I was a perpetual teenager devoid of any recognition of how to dress myself much less do anything else responsible. Hell, I now lived off a weekly allowance because they got tired of me forgetting how much money I had, and them having to clean up the effects of these lapses in memory.

Although I didn't know it the morning after our night on the back porch, I was about to assume my role in the family again. We were having breakfast together and laughing about something that happened in the town a few weeks back when I casually said, "So, you'll never guess who I ran into at the flea market yesterday."

"Then I'm not going to bother guessing," Crystal said winking at Lee as he nodded in her direction. They both laughed at this long running ritual, and I did too thinking about how nice it was to feel like we were all in sync again.

"My favorite," I said, and both of their jaws dropped off their faces. I laughed so hard at their reactions that I almost knocked the makeshift breakfast table we set up in the bed earlier in the morning to the ground. I was thoroughly pleased with myself in that moment even though by the end of the day all I would have left to be proud of was the fact that I made them breakfast – without starting any fires, thank you very much – in bed for the first time in our lives.

"No way," Crys says with incredibly wide eyes.

"Are you serious," Lee adds.

"No joke, no prank – I'm serious."

"How is that even possible," Lee asks, and Crystal pokes him in the shoulder nodding her head almost hard enough to remind me of the metal shows she enjoys.

"I don't know. I was leaving the flea market with the things I gave y'all last night and the CDs I got for me, and suddenly, there he was standing right in front of me."

"Are you sure it was him," Lee says and Crys laughs almost hard enough to knock the breakfast table onto the ground herself.

"Really Lee? Really? Of course, I'm sure it was him."

"I don't know babe, I'm sorry, but you have fooled around a lot over the years so I was making sure." Crys is having way too much fun with Lee's latest assertion of my comparatively whorish ways. I want to be offended, but I can't honestly say I would recognize all of them so maybe he does have a point, maybe just a little. I comfort myself by thinking about the fact that I now live in a place named by the owner of a whorehouse. Crystal is trying to catch her breath, and pounding on the comforter at the same time.

Composing herself, Crys says, "So what happened?"

"Nothing really. He said excuse me and I did too, and then we walked off in different directions. We both saw each other, he looked at least as shocked as I was, and that was it. It all happened in just a couple of seconds."

"That is crazy, what are you going to do babe," Lee asks.

"I don't know, but I need to find out who he is if I can."

"Isn't that against your own rules," Crys asks sarcastically wagging her finger at me like some television parent or schoolteacher. "What about all that stuff about never wanting to know who any of those people were, I mean, I don't know Jacks, what would Jackson say," and now her and Lee are both having way too much fun with this. I move the table off the bed sure their cackles and bed slapping will ultimately make a mess if I don't. I'm glad someone is enjoying this, I think, and wonder how I'm supposed to find out who he is.

"Yeah, yeah, yeah, laugh it up you two, seriously though, this is kind of a different situation with me all well known in a small town, don't you think?"

"Yeah, but it's also kind of hilarious don't you think," Lee says and Crystal nods. I nod, and in my head, I admit that from their perspective this is likely pure hilarity. From my perspective, however, this is a tricky situation.

Composing herself, Crystal says, "So, do you think he lives in Queens? What was his," she uses her fingers to make quote marks, "name again, something from the Bible right?"

"I don't know. At first, I thought he had to live here, but he might not, and his name was Paul Roman."

Lee says, "Yeah, he could be from Augusta or any of the little towns around here. He could even be on vacation traveling through the state. Either way, I don't remember anyone with that name here so if it's real he probably doesn't live here."

"There is no way that name is real," Crys says for the millionth time in the last decade, "A probably closeted guy named after the apostle who hated us in his letters, come on, if that's his real name maybe there is a god with a sense of humor out there."

Finally getting to laugh a bit myself, I ask, "So how might I find out who he is?"

Lee shakes his head, but Crystal says, "Well, start online with the name, and then when you can show Lee it's not real," she pokes Lee in the arm, "Start looking at Facebook, and stuff for people in Queens and other places near here. Since all you know is what he looks like, you're going to have to find a picture of him."

Lee says, "Yeah, pictures, oh man, you could also look at the local paper for photos, or even better, some churches in the area, even up in Augusta, have directories they published in little books when we were kids, but sometimes are available online now. You could check those out too, and see if you find your favorite face." At the use of the nickname, the two of them again collapse into giggles at my expense, and I start planning to try out their advice.

A few hours and far too many social media profiles later, I have learned a couple of things. First, Paul Roman is not the name of anyone I can find that might even potentially be my favorite. There are, apparently, people with that name, but none of them are even close. Second, searching social media without a name is not fun at all. You basically get a whole lot of pictures of food, city and town landmarks, and events. You can then try to sift through all the people that like or share or pin a given city or town, but this is also monotonous and mostly useless. Though I thought the idea sounded silly, probably due to my limited experience with small towns or churches, I finally decide to try out the church directories.

Unfortunately, most sites I find don't have member directories online best I can tell, and I am certainly not going to the churches in town in search of hard copies. I go on Facebook, and search for the local AME church by name. When I do this, I find that I can scroll through the people who 'like' the church after I 'like' it, and I start seeing many people I have seen around town and some I've talked to a lot. At some point, this feature will change, I guess, because I try it again later for another reason to no avail. At the time, however, it seems like a better approach. I'm still thinking there should be a faster way to do this and aware that I better unlike the places after I look unless I want a feed full of church news next week. I don't remember to do this, of course. I have kind of lost interest in the project, but I still want to know who he is if that is at all possible so I decide I will check out the other big church in town.

Throughout the day, I move back and forth between my den and the back porch. Crystal and Lee have been here, moving around the house and at times laughing at me some more, the whole time except for about an hour when Crys went out to walk and talk with May when she saw May passing our house. She came back smiling, and said her and May were going to meet up for coffee the next day. Lee keeps suggesting people Paul could be for fun, and then standing over me until I check to make sure he is not, for example, the mayor of Augusta, North Augusta, Waynesboro, and a few other places, or the starting shortstop for the minor league baseball team in Augusta. He is vocal in his opinion that

I am wasting my time, and I can't say I disagree with him though I won't tell him that.

When I finish with everyone I can look at from the AME church, I walk past Crystal and Lee chatting in the kitchen and sit down out on the back porch. The Baptist church will be my last passage through way too many photos that look about the same tonight. I light the third from the last remaining smoke I am not supposed to have, take a sip on the beer I grabbed before starting the latest round of searching in the den, and search for the local Baptist church on Facebook. I find it, like it, laugh at myself a little bit, and move my cursor to the people who like this page. I spend what once again feels like far too much time scrolling through the photos that all look kind of similar until, finally, I see him. There he is. Right there on the church's page. I stare at the name, the picture, and his own personal page shocked that I can be even more surprised than I was at the flea market the other day.

At this moment, Crystal and Lee come outside holding wine glasses and talking about the continuing local concerns about the pending lightning storms. It sounds like everyone is sure the end of the world is coming soon, and I wonder if I would miss the place if the town's folk are right this time. They each take seats across from me, and Crystal says, "You look like you've seen a ghost Jacks."

"Did you actually find him," Lee adds.

I look at the screen. I look at them. I exhale a somehow painful breath, and look up at the sky. I nod. I take a puff off my cigarette I'm not supposed to have. I nod again.

"What's his name," they both ask almost at the same time.

"Pastor David."

CHAPTER 21

"That is not funny Jackson," Crystal says utilizing the curse word version of my name, and placing her cigarettes on the table.

"Yeah," Lee says staring at me, "Not a good joke babe."

"No joke, I'm surprised too y'all." I get it, my favorite being the pastor at one of the bigger churches in town is not exactly the best-case scenario, especially when we know his wife is not a fan of people like us, well, people like him too I guess and chuckle a bit. At the same time, they seem more aggravated by my statement than I would have expected. It never mattered who my favorite, or any of my other companions, were before, and I don't understand why this wouldn't make a wonderful joke if it wasn't true. Hell, it sounds like the exact type of joke Crystal would come up with in other contexts.

"Jackson," I'm still a curse word, "Some things are not meant for pranks, stop playing around. Did you actually find out who it is or not," Crystal says and Lee just nods. Maybe they misinterpreted my chuckle, I wonder as I flip my computer around so they can see the screen. I figure when they see the picture they'll understand that I'm not trying to mess with them.

"I told you I'm not joking. Trust me, this would not be my first choice either, but take a look, that is him unless there is another David Matthews who is also a pastor. That is the same guy I've been seeing for years in Ybor, and the same guy I ran into at the flea market – it's him." Both stare at the screen, then look at me, then stare at the screen again, and shake their heads. They look surprised, which I can relate to, but they also look angry, and I'm not sure why they would be angry at me, him, or at us. Once again, thanks to Chuck, I feel like I'm missing some important piece of information.

"Are you sure this is him," Lee sneers at me. Well, he is angry, which is especially odd. Where did my lovable peacemaker who makes the best of everything go all the sudden? Lee is almost never angry, and when he is, it is usually because I have broken something.

I haven't broken anything in quite a while – I'm proud of this – and there is nothing here, that I can see, he will have to fix.

"You could be wrong Jackson," and now I know Crystal is pissed off at me too. That voice, I know all too well from the many times I have made her mad. Unfortunately, I am good at making Crys angry, and this is both one of the things that attracts her to me most and one of the main annoyances in her life. I know that voice, and she is ready to hurt me. Why are they so mad at me about this?

"Come on, y'all, I think I know what my favorite looks like after a decade," I say in what I hope is a friendly, fun kind of tone. I feel like I'm in trouble, a feeling I'm used to, but this time I don't understand why. They've known about the favorite for years so what is the difference now that we know who he is. This topic has always been a fun, kind of humorous, one for us, and I'm not sure why that seems to have changed. In many ways, he's also been their favorite – well, him and that Mormon missionary I found back in Miami – so I don't see what the big deal is and the shift in their tones feels especially harsh to me. At that moment, the name Paul Roman for a pastor in Georgia strikes me as kind of adorable, but I keep quiet about it because I doubt they're in the mood for adorable.

"Are you sure," they both ask at almost the exact moment, and this time they almost shout it at me. It dawns on me that I've not yet mentioned to them that I know about the existence of his sister or that the four of them were friends. Maybe their anger has something to do with why they've never mentioned these details to me. Why didn't they ever tell me about the Matthews' kids? Why did Chuck, who I especially hate in this moment, not like David? Come to think of it, why is David suddenly even cuter now that I know he is someone Chuck didn't like? Most of all, why are they so angry? I feel like I've just stumbled into a cage that was invisible only moments ago, and I get the impression there might not be any way out of it that won't be incredibly painful. I wish I could smack Chuck in the face with all my might.

"You could be wrong, a lot of people look similar, you know," Lee says sounding more like he is trying to convince himself.

Jumping aboard Lee's denial train after laughing at him when he did this kind of thing in bed earlier, Crys says, "Yeah, maybe your favorite is just someone who looks like this guy, that would make a lot more sense." I'm trying to figure out how that would make any more or less sense, but I got nothing. It is not like either of them to attempt to hide from information, and it feels striking. They made careers asking tough questions, searching for information, and looking at data. Why are they trying to ignore this?

Laughing, Lee says, "Yeah, I'm sure that's what it is. Remember when Mrs. Downey used to confuse me with that guy Lucas when we were little? It's probably something like that, Jackson's been looking all day, and just landed on something close."

This line of reasoning is starting to annoy me, but I stay quiet trying to think of a way, short of going and visiting the guy, to convince them I know what I'm talking about here. We are talking about someone I've spent a lot of time with, and I have absolutely no doubt it's the right person. I understand they obviously don't want to face this reality for some reason, but I'm at a loss as to what the big deal is. I slept with Pastor David, many times over the course of many years, so what? Okay, maybe people in town will have issues if they find out, but they already have issues and we handle it fine. What is the big deal? Why are they acting like I just told them I have an extra head they never knew about? Why are they so determined to avoid this? For a minute, I even start to wonder if I got the wrong person, but then I imagine my favorite's face in Tampa hotel rooms, and sure enough, that face belongs to Pastor David.

"That's got to be it. You're just tired Jackson, and you picked the wrong person who kind of looks like your favorite. I'm sure that's it," Crys says and finally smiles. If I used the same kind of line on her, she would shout me into oblivion for being an asshole, and true, I am starting to get tired, but only of this shit.

Sighing, I say, "I did not pick the wrong person, and I'm not that tired though I'm getting tired of this bullshit from you two," I say as calmly as I can because I can feel myself starting to get mad at them. I take a deep breath, and say, "This is him, and I don't see what the big deal is. It is him, and I'm sure that if there are any issues in town or whatever we can handle it." They are both shaking their heads again, and then it hits me. There *is* a way to stop this cycle of 'it is him' then 'we don't think so' then repeat. I have an answer for them. "Y'all were friends with him when you were younger right?"

I know they were, but I still wait for them to nod. They seem suspicious, and I guess that is understandable since the question comes out of nowhere and they haven't ever told me about this. I don't care. I just want the conversation to move forward.

"Did you ever go swimming? Hang out in locker rooms? Or do anything else where you saw him without a damn shirt on?"

They both look at me the same way they do when they think I'm up to something bad, but they also nod. Yep, they are suspicious. Good, I am up to something, but it's something good for me because it will end this shit. I just remembered that I can identify David beyond this photo if it is him that I knew in Tampa – I'm sure it is at this point even more than when I first told them – and if they have seen him without a shirt. I ask them if they are sure, and they both nod again while still looking at me with questioning eyes.

"Good, does Pastor David have a birthmark in the small of his back that looks oddly like the state of Mississippi on a map?" I remember staring at this thing so many times when we were together. It was honestly quite eerie just how strong the resemblance was. Some nights, when I was bored and not ready to go home or decide to stay the night, I would map out the cities I had been to in that state. I remembered that Long Beach would live just above the beginning of his ass crack, and giggled at the thought. I remember humming Bob Dylan's song sometimes when we were in the shower together. I remember he found it funny. "Did he have this birthmark? My favorite in Ybor sure as hell did."

I got 'em! The cycle is broken. I can tell right away that he does have it, and that they have seen it too. Their faces fall and their jaws drop like they did when I told them my favorite was at the flea market. It is him. I was right and they have nothing to say! Take that assholes, I think with a smile. Part of me wants to kind of rub it in that I was right, but I'm too relieved by their silence and worried about their anger to do so. They just sit there staring at me, at the picture, at me again, and then at each other. Lee still looks angry, but also sad for some reason, and Crystal looks like she is getting angrier by the second. I still don't know what the big deal is, but I'm glad I at least got them to stop doubting I could pick out a ten-year-long lover from a mug shot. We sit in silence. The air between us feels tense, but I wait for them to break the silence.

"How could you do that," Lee asks sounding like he is both angry and hurt. It hits me that Lee still has a crush on a preacher's son who might be Pastor David. Oh shit, I think, does this mean I slept with Lee's first love many times over the past decade and he just found out. Was I right that Pastor David was the preacher's son in question? His reaction says yes. In fact, he looks like I just punched him in the gut, and I suddenly wish I had been mistaken about the photo. I don't know what to say. I don't know what I'm supposed to say. It's not like I had any way of knowing before today, but that detail doesn't comfort me all that much with my husband looking so upset. I try to think of a response, and I fail miserably. I meet his stare hoping I'm reading his words wrong. There must be something to say, but I run out of time to do so because Crys has confusing words too.

Looking at Lee with eyes that could cut someone's heart out, and then sneering at me, Crystal says, "I can't believe you would touch that piece of shit, I thought you were better than that Jackson!" Lee looks like he's been punched in the gut again, and I don't know what she means. Crystal looks at me in a way I have never seen before, and her words and voice suggest she is disgusted with me – and maybe with Lee. Her hands are shaking, and her eyes are on fire. I've never seen her so mad, and I'm a little worried she might punch one or both of us in the next few seconds.

There is no time to respond because Crys gets up from the table cursing and heads toward the end of the driveway like she does on her walks. At the same time, Lee gets up from the table, looking like he might cry or scream or both, and heads for the door to the house. I don't know what's happening so I shout, "Aren't we going to talk about whatever the hell this is," but neither responds. Within moments, Lee is somewhere inside the house, and Crys is gone. I turn my computer around, look at the picture on the screen, and silently wonder what the hell David and I have done.

CHAPTER 22

I stayed up for a long time after they left me sitting on the back porch. I was hoping Lee would come back down, but I never saw him again. I was hoping Crys would come home from her walk, but by the time I finally went to sleep around four she had not yet done so. I wanted to talk to them, and figure out what happened on the porch. They were both angry with me. That much I could tell. I just didn't understand why. While I was awake, I studied David's social media sites, and the church's website. I found it interesting that, aside from his name and occupation and address, I had gotten to know him pretty well over the years.

When I woke up the next morning, I was alone. The house was empty, and while there were signs that the two had been there while I slept, the place just felt empty. It was around noon, and I knew that meant the lunch rush – what little rush remained – at Chuck's. Lee was probably there, but I had no clue where Crystal might be. I decided to try to get some work done, and then go up to the diner later in the afternoon. I sat out on the back porch trading emails, and doing some reading for a couple hours until Marcus called asking questions about turntables. Dante had broken the stylus on one of the ones we got him, and Marcus wanted to know how to fix it. I explained the different types to him, told him where my supplies and tools were stored at the Tampa house in case I had one he could use, and gave him the information for a shop in St. Pete that would do it for him if he needed. We spent an hour on the phone catching up on life, but I left out the current situation.

When we got off the phone, it was after five and I knew Chuck's didn't do much business these days on the weeknights. I decided to finally get dressed, and go see if my husband or wife might talk to me. When I got to Chuck's, Lee was behind the grill. He saw me come in, watched me wave, and then turned his back on me. "Trouble in paradise," Richard said.

149

"Something like that," I said, and asked if Crystal was around. Richard informed me that she had already left for the day. Lee said nothing, and Shelby kept glancing back and forth between the two of us. I was about to leave, but then I saw May sitting down in the bottom of the T and decided to say hello.

"How you doing," I said as I approached the table with a cup of coffee Shelby had given me at the bar.

May looked up from the notepad they were writing on, and said, "Oh, hey Jackson, I'm good, really good. Crystal and I had a long talk earlier, and she was telling me about some scholarship options and that maybe I could live in your old house when I moved to Tampa." I was glad to see that Crystal wasn't mad at everyone after last night. I also thought about how great it would be both for May to have a stable place to live, and one with a damn genius next door at that. I was willing to bet that a couple years of chats with Deidre would have May leaving us all – even Crystal – in the dust intellectually based on what I'd seen so far from them.

"It is a nice place, and you'd probably really like the neighbors a lot too."

"It sounds like a dream."

"Nothing wrong with having some dreams," I say and sit down across the table.

"I think I'm starting to agree with that. Crystal said I wouldn't have to pay rent as long as I was willing to take care of the place and be respectful when someone named Marcus needed it."

"Marcus is one of the neighbors you'd probably like. He is probably the best friend I've ever had, and a lot of fun. He lives next door with his wife Deidre, who is an engineer and about the smartest person you'll ever meet, and their son Dante. Sometimes Marcus uses the house for various reasons, and so if you're there, you'll just have to be open to that and maybe even attend some of his parties."

"That sounds fun."

"They are, sometimes, and that is coming from someone who doesn't often like parties. Crystal is right though, there would be no reason for you to pay rent. Use your money for school, and if you transition, for that. We have enough for now."

"I don't know how to thank y'all," May says with a big grin.

"You don't need to, we remember being young and different and just want to help however we can."

"Lee even gave me some contacts down there, some people he knows."

"They're good people, and like everyone else, they basically adore Lee and will take good care of you when you're living there. They actually taught Lee a lot about trans issues over the years, and might be able to help you if you want tips for dealing with your family and others who might not be so open minded."

"That's what Lee was saying."

May and I keep chatting at the table until they leave around eight o'clock. At that point, I consider heading home, but decide to stay since the diner closes at nine tonight and I want to see if Lee will at least talk to me about what he's feeling. I call Crystal on her cell phone hoping for the same chance, but she doesn't answer. I watch the last few customers of the night come in and go out over the next hour. Lee cooks and chats with people like he would on any other day, but he seems quieter and more hesitant than usual. Just after nine, the last customer leaves and Lee sends Shelby home saying he'll take care of the mess. He looks in my direction as he says this, and for a minute, I wonder if he'll ask me to leave for once.

I sit there for a few minutes watching Lee shut down the grill and clean various parts of the area behind the bar. He doesn't ask me to leave, but he doesn't speak to me either. I've been here at closing many times now, and this is not the way it usually goes. I decide to pretend it's a normal night so I start cleaning up where I am, and working my way up the bottom of the T. Using the materials Lee keeps down in the table busting station in the bottom corner of the T, I clean the tables, wipe the seats, and put the seats on the tables. When I'm done, I clean the floor. Lee is still working behind the bar. I see him smile, just a little bit, as I finish the bottom portion of the T and begin wiping down the jukebox with my rag. An old Madonna song plays, and I shake my hips while singing along. He walks back into the kitchen, and I begin cleaning the booths on the top of the T.

As I start to work on the booths on the left side of the top line of the T, he comes out of the kitchen, through the swinging door, and says, "You're not making it easy to hate you as much as I want to right now Jacks." Lee always loves it when I help him close the place since he knows how much I hate dirty stuff – and he really loves it when I dance – and I admit I'm using this to my advantage. I just need him to talk to me no matter how mad he needs to be.

"I guess that's fair since I don't even know what you're mad about this time."

Sighing, he says, "I honestly don't know either because the logical part of me knows I have no real right to be mad at you."

"Is my always so kind spouse admitting that maybe he's being unfair for once?"

"Probably," he says and stops cleaning the kitchen area. He pours himself a cup of coffee, and asks if I want one. I accept the offer, and he points to one of the booths near the office Crystal uses. I meet him there, and we sit down. Sighing again, he says, "Look, it's not fair for any number of reasons, but it really bothers me that you've been sleeping with David for the last decade. Hell, the thought of you sleeping with him once bothers me a lot."

"Okay," I say sipping from my cup. "I get that, and it's pretty obvious my love, but why does it bother you so much? Is David the preacher's son you fell in love with when you were younger? Do you still have feelings for him? It seemed that way on your birthday last year, and with some of your comments lately. Is that the issue?"

Lee takes a sip of his coffee, and asks, "Do you have a smoke by chance?"

"Really?"

"Yeah, I think I could use one for this."

"I should remind you this is a non-smoking restaurant sir," I say imitating his own statement to me a few days before when I said Chuck's would be perfect if I could just smoke while we cleaned up at night.

"Shut up," he says sounding like my husband again, smiling, and taking the cigarette I hand him. I get up from the table, and go into the office where I know Crys keeps an ashtray from back when people could smoke in the restaurant. When I come back with it, Lee says, "Ha, I didn't know she had this, it's from when we were kids."

"Yeah, she told me she found it in a file cabinet. She doesn't use it, but she likes having it. I guess that means we'll have to wash it when we're done." I light Lee's cigarette, and he coughs for a few seconds before getting the hang of it again. He was never much of a smoker, and I've only seen him have a few in all the time I've known him. "So, what's up?"

"You're right, David is the one I was talking about, but there is more to it than that."

"I figured."

"David and I were best friends the whole time we were growing up here. We spent like every day together as kids, and were kind of inseparable – like Crys and I when you met us. He was my first kiss, my first close friend, I mean, he was basically everything to me until our senior year of high school. My feelings for him were, and hell I guess still are, the only thing that has ever been on the same kind of level the three of us have now."

"I can understand that. Why didn't you ever tell me this before?"

"I don't know Jacks, it got all complicated. When we got to high school, we started hanging out with Crystal because she was best friends – and I later learned more than that – with his sister Autumn. Him and Crys were even close when we were sophomores and juniors. His little sister was a year behind us, and they were close so he kept an eye on her and brought her to any party or function we went to. She was really, and I mean really, shy, but also cool, you know, you would have liked her a lot."

"So that was Autumn Matthews, and she was more than just best friends with Crys?"

"Yeah, that was her, Autumn, and yeah she was for Crys what David was for me. How did you know her name, did Crys tell you about her?"

"Nope. I saw Crys on one of her walks when I went out one evening, and she was over at the cemetery not far from here. She didn't see me because she left before I got close enough, but I found the spot she was at, it had one of those tulips she loves on the grave, and Autumn's name was there. I then learned from Miss Ruby about the friendship and Autumn's suicide."

"Yeah, the suicide was tough. Crys was a wreck, and wanted to get out of here so bad. That's why we went to Tallahassee instead of Augusta. It was hard on David too, and he had some issues for a couple years afterward. He went to Bible College because his father wanted him too, and he ended up liking it. We traded letters for a couple years, but it was hard to stay in touch like that."

"Is Autumn why Crystal likes those tulips so much?"

"Yeah, they were her favorites, and Crys used to tease her about them when they were at the beginning of high school because Autumn said she wanted to live in a house made of tulips. You know, kid's stuff I guess."

"So, what happened between the four of you?"

Sighing and wiping a tear from his face, Lee says, "It's complicated, but by the end of sophomore year Crystal and I started having feelings for each other. We both also still had feelings for David and Autumn. Anyhow, it all started because David and I almost got caught kissing, and the four of us came up with a cover story. Crys and I would pretend to be a thing to shield the rest of us, but then at a party we fooled around and realized we liked each other like that too. It was no big deal at first, and David and Autumn were both very supportive of Crys and I spending more time together and stuff. Neither one of them got it, I mean they were both mono, you know just gay and lesbian not bi, they loved us and we loved them so we all were open with each other about everything. It was kind of nice even though it was confusing for all of us at the time."

Lee puts out his cigarette, and stares out the window for a few minutes. I just stay silent, and wait for him. I can tell this isn't easy for him, and I don't want to push. While I'm at least starting to understand his reaction last night, Crys' reaction is only getting even more confusing with every good thing I learn about the David formerly known as "favorite." I try to imagine the four of them roaming around this town, getting drinks in this diner, and growing up back then. I wonder what that was like. They had to hide, just like I did, but they did have others in hiding with them, and I felt like that had to make a lot of difference. Lee motioned toward my pack, and I handed him another cigarette. He lit it, and coughed again.

After another puff, he started again, "Everything was really great you know. I mean, it wasn't perfect because we had to keep quiet, and I was the only one anybody knew about. Like I told you before, I accidentally came out one night to Thelma and the year I almost got caught. The time when I talked to Thelma, well, that was a big one. It was after the first time David and I almost had sex, and I freaked out bad, so did he. We didn't speak for like three weeks, and it felt like forever. Aside from that, though, everything was good, and we had a plan. The four of us were going to go to Augusta for college or maybe down to Thomasville if Autumn needed to get away from here, and get a house together. It was our big dream, and we were all planning for it until homecoming senior year."

"What happened?"

"I don't really know for sure. Crys won't talk about it, and David wouldn't back then so I'm not sure. Somehow, David's parents found out about Autumn, and they took her out of school. They also grounded David, and he didn't get to leave the house or the church until he left for Bible College the following summer. We only spoke one more time before we each left town, and then we traded a few letters in college. I don't know what all happened, but Autumn was home-schooled after winter break our senior year, and then in the middle of March of that year, she killed herself. Crystal might know more, but she's never said so, and anyway, Autumn's death kind of changed everything for us."

"How so?"

"Crystal always blamed David for some reason, and she really just started hating him as time went by. I asked her about it back then, but she never offered a reason. The best guess I could come up with was that she thought David outed Autumn to the family, but I doubt that would have happened. In any case, he became public enemy number one in Crys' mind after Autumn died, and even a little bit before she died. She would get angry just at the mention of him, and she still does. Remember us fighting a while back, those fights were because she asked me about the religion stuff, and I admitted I was thinking of contacting David, and maybe trying to get back in touch. She got so angry at the idea, and I got so angry at her reaction that we barely spoke for a few days just like happened when we were younger."

"I wondered what the hell was going on with you two."

"Yeah, I'm sorry for being so distant, and I bet Crys feels the same way. Some of this stuff is just still so hard to talk about."

"So, you had to choose between David and Crystal?"

"It wasn't much of a choice honestly. David was going to Bible College, and the only time we got close to having sex we both freaked out, so I interpreted his silence that spring to mean he wasn't interested in me anymore. I didn't know I was wrong about that until I was already in Tallahassee. I knew I loved Crys, and I knew I wanted to have real, you know open, relationships with men someday. I didn't think David could, or would, offer that, and I knew Crys could and would love and accept all of me whether we stayed together or not romantically or as friends. We went to Florida and left all this behind, but I never really got over David."

"So, when you found out my favorite was David, you felt like I'd taken your first love from you or something like that?"

"Kind of," he says tapping ashes from his cigarette, "That's kind of how it feels, and it makes me want to hurt you. But there is more to it, I think. I think I'm jealous that you got something I've wanted my whole life, but I also think I'm hurt that he was in Tampa every year, right down the road from me, in bed with my husband, but he never contacted me even though everyone here in town knew I lived down there. Part of me has wanted to see if there is still something there since I got back to town, but now I wonder if I meant anything to him at all."

"I can understand that. You should know that I won't touch him again unless you say so, and I am sorry that the news has caused you so much anguish."

"I appreciate that Jacks."

"What do you want to do?"

"I don't know. I'll probably keep being mad at you for a little while longer, and I have a feeling I'll feel like shit for that later."

"Stay mad as long as you need, but please don't give up on us if you can help it."

"I won't, you know I love y'all with all I got. Right now, I just kind of want to hate you a little bit too."

"I can understand that, I've been happily hating Chuck since the night Crys told me y'all wanted to move up here."

Laughing, Lee says, "I figured as much when you weren't angry with either of us." He smiles, and continues, "As for David and Crystal, I don't know what I'll do, but that's not new at this point. I think I'll just need some time to myself."

"Just know I'll be here if you need me," I say with a smile and he nods and wipes his eyes again. He smiles at me for a second, and then looks out the window again. "Do you want me to get out of here and give you some space," I ask.

"Yeah," he says with a heavy voice, "I think that would be good."

CHAPTER 23

"You have a lot of nerve to show up here," Crystal says as she approaches Autumn's grave. After my conversation with Lee, I walked over here hoping I would see her at some point. I've been sitting here for a couple hours when she arrives, and she does not appear happy to see me in the least. I am still replaying all the details of Lee's stories when she arrives, and I'm kind of glad she speaks first because I don't know what to say.

"I thought that's what you loved about me – my inability to recognize when I'm doing something foolish," I say lighting a smoke, and watching her silhouette in the moonlight.

She stares down at me in a way that can't be healthy for me, and then sighs. "What do you want," she says in short, clipped syllables that usually mean she is in no mood for my shenanigans. Although I don't think I've ever seen her so mad at me, I am comforted by how familiar I am with angry Crys in this moment.

"I just want to understand."

"And if I don't want to talk," she asks in those same short syllables.

"Then I'll see you here again tomorrow night I guess."

"Why do you have to be so difficult?"

"I learned it from watching you," I say remembering when she camped out at my bedroom door in Tampa after I got my first few rejections for books, I had been sulking for a couple weeks, and she had been patient, she made sure to tell me that twice, but enough was enough and she was going to shadow me until I talked about how I was feeling. I told her to go to hell, went into my room, and shut the door behind me. When I came back out a few hours later, she was still sitting there, leaning against the wall beside the doorway this time, and smiling up at me. Aggravated as hell, I started talking about my feelings.

"Jerk," she says probably remembering the same thing or another occasion where she pushed me to talk after waiting for me to do so on my own.

"You can talk to me now or later, but calling me names won't do you any good," I said and she just stared at me. I was quoting her word for word, and we both knew it. We also knew that if there was anyone on the planet as stubborn as she was, it was me.

After a few seconds, she sighs, and says, "Okay Jackson," and I smile because even though my name is a curse word again, at least she is talking to me. "Did you bring that," she says pointing at the fresh tulip on Autumn's grave.

"Yes mam." I stopped by the house after talking with Lee to see if she was home, and grab one of the tulips if she was not.

"Did Lee tell you about this place?"

"Nope, I saw you here when I was out for a walk a while back. I also learned you were best friends with this girl and David in high school from asking around town. Lee did tell me the meaning behind the tulips, and that Autumn wasn't just a friend."

"Well aren't you the little detective," she says trying to still sound mad, but there is a hint of humor in her voice that gives me hope. I marvel at the little intricacies you get used to in a spouse's voice after years of arguments and laughter.

"You always said I could have been a researcher too."

Sighing, she sits down with her legs crossed to the right of me but also across from me, and reaches out to touch the tombstone. She smiles as she touches it, but then her face kind of drops in a swift motion, and she chokes up. She has left a good couple feet between the two of us so I make no effort to touch her just in case the space is necessary for her. Even so, a part of me aches for how close we normally sit when we're having a conversation. She places her own tulip on the grave, whispers a few words I don't catch, and wipes a tear from her eye. She looks at me, and for the first time since the back porch her eyes don't seem convinced of my pending doom. I am hoping this is a good sign. She grabs her forehead with her left hand and moves it down the length of her face before beginning to tug on her lip. She lets out a deep breath, and finally says, "She wasn't just a friend," before pulling out a pack of cigarettes.

"What was she like?"

She sniffs a little bit and lights a smoke. She shakes her shoulders just a little like she's trying to get something off her body, and says, "She was perfect Jacks. No one really knew her all that much because she was so quiet. She spent most of her time reading every book she could get her hands on and trying to figure out everything in the whole world," she smiles and chuckles. A little bit of color returns to her face, and she says, "She thought life was a joke, and she had the same whimsical quality you do that made it hard to take things too seriously when you were around her. She just radiated optimism and fun. One day she would be certain she was going to join the circus when she grew up, and the next day she was going to be an astrophysicist. She was always dreaming adventures we should take. Life was an adventure, and she wanted all of it all the time. I can't explain it, but she kind of inspired me if that makes any sense." She sniffs again, and chuckles for a second, "Honestly, I don't really know how to put her into words even now. She was just, I don't know, something more than just alive, and her optimism and passion was just infectious I guess. She was perfect."

"How did y'all meet?"

"I was seven and I remember I had a scarf wrapped around my hair. I was in the paper shop downtown, the one Sylus runs now, you know." I nod and she continues, "I was playing with the construction paper making Miss Betty, she was Sylus' mom, a picture, and she came bouncing in the store to get a new journal. She was wearing mismatched clothes and a little orange headband, and I just couldn't take my eyes off her. She told Miss Betty that she wanted the best, most sparkly journal ever, and Miss Betty found her this purple one with glitter on the cover. She jumped up and down and kept saying glitter for a few seconds. It was like nothing I'd ever seen. While Miss Betty was ringing her up, she looked over at me and said, 'You're pretty, I like you, I'm Autumn like the Fall, who are you.' Just like that, no pretense, no sense really, she just started talking to me out of nowhere, and I started laughing so hard Jacks." She smiles at me or maybe she just looks at me while smiling at the memory. "I told her my name, and she said, 'I like that, let's be friends,' and from then on, we were and I got my first journal because I wanted to be like her that day."

"So y'all knew each other for most of childhood?"

"Yeah, from that day we were kind of a unit," she says chuckling, "We were always together, and she would call me 'the pretty Crystal' and I would call her 'my favorite season' in notes we passed. We were just kids then, but I think we already felt something special. She was a grade below me, but we spent all our spare time together at school and at the diner. Later, when we were in high school, we both started having all kinds of feelings that were confusing and good at the same time. I was in ninth grade when she gave me a note that said she loved me, and I carried that little note around for two weeks in my pocket."

She chuckles for a second, and then continues, "David used to look after her back then because she got picked on a lot. She was quiet, strange, and loved her books, and for some kids, that made her a target. It was especially bad when she was in eighth grade so when she came to high school, we started hanging out with David and Lee all the time. The son of the preacher and the football star did not get picked on, and suddenly, we were safe and free in and out of school. We would go everywhere with David and Lee, and that's kind of how Lee and I first got close back then. We would just hang out alone or with the boys every day. The four of us had a lot of fun together in high school until senior year when it all fell apart."

"What happened senior year," I asked, but she kind of closed in on herself like she was afraid so I leaned back away from her and said, "It's okay if it's too hard to talk about Crys." Her body opened just a little bit, and she looked at me with a softness in her eyes.

"No," she said, "We should probably have talked about this long before now. I'm sure you could tell how angry I was at you the other night." She was right. Her anger the other night felt like it bled out of every pore in her body, and I was still stinging a little bit.

"I could, and honestly, it kind of felt like you were disgusted with me."

"I was," she says and sighs. "The thought of you with him just really bothers me. Of all the people in the world, I just can't make sense of you with him. I know Lee loves him, and always has, but the guy is just terrible Jackson, he's just the worst."

"Lee says you blame him for Autumn's death, but he doesn't know why. I would think a person I blamed for my first love's death would be about the worst in my book too. I mean, even now after all this time, the thought of someone hurting River makes me want to fight, and I know from Facebook that he is safe and raising a family with his wife out in Oregon not in the ground somewhere so I can only imagine how you feel."

"I blame him because he fucking killed her," she sneers with more hatred in her voice than I would have thought possible. I was half expecting to learn the next day that David dropped dead from the impact. Her whole face changed, and she seemed like a completely different person as those words left her mouth. If I'm being completely honest, she scared me in that moment like no one ever had, and I felt afraid for David's safety. I felt like her anger could consume the whole cemetery, and I distinctly remember fighting the urge to run and hide. "He fucking killed her Jackson," she repeated again, and threw out her cigarette.

Speaking softly and slowly, attempting to keep my voice level, I said, "What do you mean by that Crys?" I knew from talking to Ruby that Autumn killed herself in her parents' home. There seemed to be no debate about this so I wasn't sure what Crys was talking about. Was she saying the facts reported were wrong, or was she saying that David was part of the reason that Autumn took her life? I couldn't tell.

"I mean he killed her, or, I mean, he's the reason she's dead."

"How did he cause her death," I asked.

"It was the night of homecoming, and we were celebrating the game and my new crown. The four of us were hanging out at first after the dance at a party another kid was throwing, but then we went off in our separate directions during the party. The party was out at the lake, and I don't know what David and Lee got into that night, but Autumn and I went down to the shore to be alone. We probably should have been more careful that night. We were always so careful before that night except when we were around Lee because he already knew we were more than friends. Lee didn't care. He was in love with David, and thought what we had was basically the same thing, no better or worse. Lee and I were also together at times by this point, and we had this agreement about protecting our respective loves. So, we weren't worried about Lee. David didn't know, and no one else knew. We were sitting in a little patch of grass, like you and I are now, just talking and kissing and hanging out. It was getting close to their curfew, but we didn't notice because we were so happy wrapped up in each other."

Crystal lights another smoke, and stares off into the distance for a little while. She is pulling on her lip again, and taking deep breaths. Her shoulders are shaking and her body is closing in on itself again. "Are you okay," I ask, and she nods, but doesn't say anything at first. She takes a few more long breaths, and a couple puffs on her cigarette and looks back at me. She has tears running down her face, and keeps sniffling in between breaths. She shakes her shoulders again before she starts to speak.

"We were kind of making out, nothing much but the most we had done with each other at that point so kind of a big deal for us. David came to get her so they wouldn't miss curfew, and walked into the grassy area as we were mouth to mouth with our bodies pressed tightly into each other. We didn't hear him. We didn't know he was there. We were too wrapped up in each other to notice anything. It was a magical night, I mean, I was the homecoming queen and we loved each other and I had Lee too at that point. Everything that year seemed like a dream, like the world was smiling on me somehow. At some point, we heard David say, 'Woah,' and suddenly we knew he was there. We moved away from each other quickly, but we knew he had seen us. He turned his back to us as he said, 'We gotta get home sis, or we're going to be late,' and Autumn kissed me one more time. She was fearless, but I was not, I was already worried about what might happen. It was our last kiss, but I didn't know it then. As we walked, a few yards behind David, back to where our cars and Lee were waiting, she told me not to worry about it, but I felt scared. She was sure that David didn't care, but I was worried she was wrong about him and about how our families would react."

"Then what happened," I ask after a few seconds.

"He told his parents about us when they got home."

"How do you know that?"

"Because they called my parents the next morning, and told them about us. That was when my parents sat me down and talked to me about sexuality, which I think I told you about years ago, right?"

"Yeah, you told me that, but never how they knew."

"They knew because David told, and his parents told mine."

"How do you know he told them?"

"No one else could have Jackson," she says turning my name into a synonym for stupid. "We were so careful all the time, and they found out right after he saw us that night. The only explanation, after I thought about it in every way over the years, is that he told on us for some reason even though we never told on him or Lee even after that night." Her hands shake, her face adopts a hardened look, and she continues, "He told his parents, and they lost it. I mean, they went crazy," she says as more tears roll down her cheeks. "They pulled Autumn out of school, and started having daily prayer sessions, they called it homeschool. It wasn't home school, it was prison and she was trapped," she says shaking even harder than before, and wiping the tears from her eyes. "She told me about it in a letter I got in the mail right after she died. She told me about it all. She said it was hell, and they kept telling her she was sick and needed help. She couldn't take it, it was too much, and so she killed herself. He told his parents, and she took her own life to get away from them. For me, that means he killed her plain and simple."

She was shaking from head to toe, and crying hard now. I think I would have been too if I was her. I couldn't imagine what that must have been like for Autumn or for Crys. It sounded like a nightmare come to life. Her hatred for David made sense, and I wondered why she had never told Lee this part of the story. I wondered how Lee would react to this information. He was in love with David, but he was also utterly opposed to anyone being treated poorly for any reason. What would he say if he knew this?

I also wondered why David got in trouble with his parents too if all he did was out his sister to them. Maybe they punished him just in case he got any ideas from her, or maybe they wondered about him before and that was part of the reason he sold his sister down the river. Why would he do that to his sister? Why would he get in trouble for it?

How could he live with himself after that? I didn't know the answers to any of these questions, but they kept repeating in my head. No matter the answers, I couldn't disagree with Crystal's assessment that anyone who did that would be just plain horrible. I wondered how painful it must have been for Crys. How do people ever fully come back from such horrendous losses?

I tried to think of something poignant or at least useful to say, but all I could come up with was, "I'm sorry Crys, that must have been terrible." Her repeated trips to this place made a lot more sense, and her issues with women when relationships got "too serious" also started to make a lot of sense. I was kind of amazed she had been able to be in any kind of long-term relationship after losing Autumn.

"He killed her Jackson, and that's the thing. I know Lee is still in love with him all these years later, but he is the one person that is off limits if Lee wants us to stay together. I just can't do that. I can't have him in my life. I don't even like to know he still exists. So, when you told us he was "the favorite," I just, I don't know Jacks, I just really felt sick inside and angry at the same time at the thought of him touching my husband."

"I can understand that."

"I know I can't tell you what to do, but I can't be with you if you're going to keep seeing him, I just don't think I can do that." She starts crying hard again, and I really want to put my arms around her. I resist the urge because she is moving even further from me, and once again, I don't want to violate her personal space. Like me, Crys has always been very serious about personal space, and so I just sit there while she cries for a few minutes.

When she starts to seem a little calmer, I say, "You don't have to worry about that Crys. I already told Lee I wouldn't touch him again because of their love thing, and this information only cements that. I wouldn't trade you or Lee for anything in the world, and I have no problem keeping my hands off David or anyone else."

"I'd understand if you felt differently, and I wouldn't try to hold you back Jacks."

"I know, and I'd understand if you see me differently now and need to have some space or distance for a while or long term." I mean it when I say this, but I also know that losing her or Lee would be my own worst nightmare. I feel like I need to give her a way out, but I also hope with all I am that she doesn't want it.

"I know, but I don't think it will come to that," she says and I celebrate inside. "As mad as I am, you didn't know who he was or what he had done to me back then. If you are okay without him, it'll all be okay with some time I think." I feel myself start to breathe again, and take a few long breaths of my own before responding.

"I hope so," I say as she reaches out her hand and I take it in mind. We stay out there for a couple more hours talking about her time with Autumn, Lee's feelings for David, and the ways coming to Queens have influenced our lives in such a short time. Later, we walk hand in hand back to the house, and say goodnight at the stairs on the first floor. She goes up to bed or maybe to journal about Autumn or other things. I go into my den, put on my headphones, and listen to music before falling asleep with my favorite blanket.

CHAPTER 24

After my long conversations in the diner and the cemetery, I went to sleep hoping to spend hours wrapped in oblivion. It had been an emotional few days, and I just needed to rest. The plan as I fell asleep involved sleeping for as long as I possibly could, and then spending the day reading or playing on the computer on the back porch. I just needed a break from other people. I wanted to take some time to reflect on everything Crys and Lee said the night before. Just a little bit of sleep and time alone, I thought as I drifted off to dream, and everything will be fine. It was a good plan, one I used at many confusing points in my life, but it was not meant to be. Instead, I woke to the sound of someone pounding on our door at about nine o'clock the next morning.

I stumbled to the doorway wiping the not enough sleep from my eyes, and looked out the peephole. The rest of the house seemed empty, and I figured that meant the others were up at the diner or off doing some morning errands. Through the little piece of glass, I saw the lady who had been in Jenny's bookshop the day I visited. She had the same angry expression she wore that day, and I realized I had not bothered to try to learn who she was at the time, but Crystal said her name was Barb. She was pounding on my door with her right hand, and holding what looked like a trash bag in her left. I stood there for a second, and considered ignoring her until she went away or at least until I had a cup of coffee. In hindsight, this might have been the smartest plan, but my curiosity overruled my concerns.

I opened the door slowly, and asked, "May I help you?"

While I was speaking, she shoved the trash bag at me with surprising force, and spat the words, "You can help me by staying away from my daughter and keeping your evil smut to yourself!"

Bewildered and barely awake, I didn't catch the bag as it bounced off my chest and fell to the floor. It was a typical black kitchen bag so I could not see what was inside, and I had no clue what the lady was talking about. "What," I managed to say before she spoke again.

"You heard me, stay away from my little girl and keep your smut to yourself. My daughter doesn't need some fancy city homo putting all kinds of evil thoughts in her head. She's a good girl and I won't see her corrupted by the likes of you and your kind." She was pointing her finger in my face the whole time, but all I noticed was the shiny cross bouncing up and down on her sternum as she spoke. Who the hell was this lady and why was she waking me up so damn early in the morning to rant about some kid?

"What kid, what smut, what are you talking about," I finally managed to say. I wished I had not answered the door, or that I at least made a cup of coffee first. "Who are you lady," I added trying to get my brain to wake up.

"Don't play dumb with me Jackson," she said and I noted that she was good at using my name as a curse word. She poked me in the chest with her skinny little white finger, and said, "I know you're the one that has been feeding my little girl unholy thoughts about sex and sin and trying to turn my little angel into a dirty tranny like the ones on TV that hurt innocent people trying to use the bathroom. I found your little stash," she says pointing at the bag at my feet, "Under her bed last night, and I know she got it from you people!" She continues to point her finger at me like a school teacher, but this is at least beginning to make sense. I'm thinking this must be May's mother when she continues, "I will not stand by while you infect my little girl with your sickness so you better stay away from her."

The neurons in my brain are finally beginning to work again. I'm still not all there, but I have an idea of what must be happening. Somehow, May's mother has found out about their study of transitioning and located the materials I provided on the subject. Rather than loving her child unconditionally, the lady has decided that there is something wrong with May, and picked me to be the scapegoat for her rage. Okay, I think, I've got this. I've seen it many times in relation to gay, lesbian, bi, asexual and trans kids before, and I know the basics. Reasoning with her likely won't do any good, quoting her own Bible will likely just make her angrier, and educating her on the history and beauty of transgender experience will likely only get me smacked and May even worse. There is no good way to handle this situation that I've ever seen, and so I figure I will at least try to get through to her in some way.

"There is nothing wrong with your child, mam, May is feeling things that many people feel, and all I've done is try to be supportive when they've come to me for advice." It takes a lot of effort to keep calm when someone is spewing hateful ignorance at you, especially if you're not fully awake, but luckily, I have way too much practice with this. My thoughts drift to May, and I hope with all my might that they are okay this morning. I also think of the times River experienced this kind of shit from his family and so called friends before and while we were together. My thoughts also land on Autumn, and I wonder if this moment is reminiscent of her own experience. I try to push that thought away with all my might but it keeps coming back like a mean-spirited boomerang.

"Don't give me any of that liberal garbage, my daughter is sick and instead of helping her you're trying to make her worse," she spits at me. "Don't let me see you near her, you hear me, or there'll be serious trouble. Some of us still have morals in this town!"

I've never understood the moral value of rejecting a child or other human being, and yet, I've heard this kind of phrasing my whole life in coffee shops, on television shows, in the news, at churches, and especially in moments where a parent learned a child was not heterosexual, mono-sexual, monogamous or cisgender for the first time. It always seemed odd to me that many parents only loved their children under certain conditions, and just as easily discarded them if they turned out some way the parent did not expect. It often seemed like people with children only wanted those children if the kids did everything exactly as they planned without too much trouble. This, I was sure, did not have much to do with morality, but rather, it seemed to be much more about control than anything else.

Smiling at the lady still staring at me with daggers in her eyes, I said, "Look, your kid is trying to figure out who they are and they have questions. I'm not going to turn them away just because you don't care enough about them to accept them for who they are."

"She is NOT MY KID, SHE IS MY DAUGHTER, and SHE WILL ALWAYS BE MY LITTLE GIRL NOT SOME WEIRD THEY,"

May's mom yells at me, and for a minute there, I think she might hit me. I'm struck by how much more important her version of May is than the actual May who lives and breathes and thinks for themselves. "We have put up with you people in town despite your lifestyles, but our children is where we draw the line!" She is shaking with rage, and I wonder just how many people in her group now have my little family at the top of their hit list. Most of them probably did before this, I'm quite sure, but maybe we have hit the limit of polite tolerance and dirty looks. For the millionth time, I wish I could beat up Chuck for putting me in this position, but at the same time, part of me is happy to be here for May.

"Whatever you call your kid, May is 18, finished with high school, and accepted to college. May can talk to whoever they want, and if you don't change your tune you might not know May for much longer." Even as I say the words, I know they'll only make her angrier. However, the conversation is getting old, and only going in circles so at this point I'm simply trying to hurry up and end it. This lady is not likely to change her opinion, and there is nothing I can do about that. I'll be better off alerting Lee, Crystal, Ruby, Lacey, and Kate so we can be ready to help May anyway we can.

My attempt to end the conversation is successful. In response, she simply grunts and sneers, "Stay away from my little girl," before turning on her heel and walking out of my yard and across the street toward downtown. I pick up the bag, and open it to reveal the books on Transgender experience and the pamphlets on gender transition I had given May. Her mom had apparently been so offended that she took the time to rip up some of the pamphlets while she stuffed them into the trash bag. I wonder where May is, and hope they are doing okay in the face of what has to be a suddenly even more hostile home. I want a shower. I want a coffee. I want to go back to sleep. Instead, I throw on some more clothes, grab my bag, and head up to the diner to update Crystal and Lee on what happened so we can get ready for whatever might follow.

"You missed the fireworks this morning," Richard says to me as I enter the diner a few minutes later looking for Lee and Crystal.

"What do you mean?"

"Jenny, Linda, Barb and some of the other ladies from the church came in here and gave your spouses a good yelling at about that girl May that comes in here all the time." He sips his coffee, and Doris nods. He continues, "It was quite the sight, May's mom, you know, Barb, well, she was especially entertaining trying to convince Lee and Crystal that they were evil and better watch out, I thought Crystal was going to jump over the counter and beat them up."

I stand there soaking in the details and wondering why the rest of them didn't come with Barb to my house. Doris says, "They think little May is one of them transgenders, but instead of helping her, they got all mad at y'all about it. It was strange." Despite her unfamiliarity with the language, Doris does her usual job of cutting right to the heart of the matter. Instead of embracing May, Barb and the crew are looking for someone to blame.

"Are Lee and Crys here?"

"Yeah, they been over in the office since the ladies left," says Shelby, and Richard, Doris, and Matt all nod. "It's kind of nice to see them talking to each other again after the last couple days, we was starting to wonder if y'all were okay."

"We're okay, just a whole lot going on these days," I say and head for the office.

When I enter the office, they are sitting across from each other with the desk in between them. The office is just a tiny room with file cabinets and clutter surrounding an old metal desk with one seat on the side with the computer, and two other chairs on the other side. Crys looks up as I enter, and says, "It's Autumn all over again, we can't let them hurt May," and Lee even puts his arm around my shoulder as I sit down beside him on the other side of the desk. For a moment, I think about how funny it is that no matter the other conflicts in our family, a crisis always bring us together immediately.

"What do you think they'll do," I ask aware that they know these people and this town much better than I do.

"David said that his parents would beat Autumn and force her to pray with them in the months after they found out about her," Lee says shaking just a little bit and looking as frightened as I think we all felt. "These people have about the same beliefs David's parents did back then so I would expect a similar reaction from them."

"And David's wife was with them this morning, and her and Barb grew up together in that fundamentalist church over on the outskirts of Milledgeville. It's the place that got in trouble when we were kids for abuses against children, remember Lee, and I think both of their families are still part of that church. They might try to send May there." Even I, the newcomer, had already heard about the church in question. It was one of those places that still believed that interracial dating, dancing, and alcohol were evil. One of those places where girls might get beaten or worse for wearing pants, and the men ruled with an iron fist and an appreciation for corporal punishment. I knew May's mom and David's wife were from Milledgeville, but I didn't realize they had come out of that church. I was starting to understand Linda's reported dichotomy between her public self and her private reading habits. She grew up in a place where repression and secrets were key, and never managed to escape.

"So, what do we do," I asked, and we spent the next couple hours outlining options. We looked at all the possible scenarios in the ways people trained in fiction, journalism, and research can, and came up with a list of options to talk to May about. Throughout the process, Crys mentioned Autumn a few more times, and each time I could tell that Lee was thinking the same thing I was – we had to try just in case we could make the story end differently this time. As we went through each option, I wondered where May was and how they were doing. I marshaled every bit of hope I had that they were okay, but I kept getting a sinking feeling in my stomach.

CHAPTER 25

About two weeks after my surprise visit from Barb, I found myself driving to Augusta for a meeting I never would have imagined before moving to Queens. With the approval of my family, I reached out to Pastor David online just in case there was anything he could do to help May or calm the anger of his parishioners. I didn't know if it was a good idea, but Lisa seemed to think highly of his work in Augusta with the support groups, and we wanted to expend every possible resource for May. After a few days, I got a message back saying he was already into it on his end, and asking if we could meet to talk about "other stuff" sometime. After talking it over with Crys and Lee, I agreed to meet him for a drink.

I arrived at the address my phone told me to go to, and sat in the car for a few minutes. The chosen place was the same shop I got a mocha when Lee and I came to town a while back, and I watched the people moving around the streets. David requested this place because it was out of the way – read not likely to draw Queens' attention – and comfortable – read potentially safe for people like us. It was a little coffee shop blended with a pub called the Metro, but as I noticed the first time I was here, it looked more like a bar that sold some coffee too. I sat in the car half listening to the Kasey Chambers album playing on my stereo, and trying to figure out what I would say to favorite, Paul, David when we sat down together.

I mean, come on, what do you talk about with your former casual lover who your husband is in love with and who may have been responsible for the death of your wife's first love? What do you talk about when it also turns out the guy happens to be the pastor of the biggest church in the small town you recently moved to with your family? If there is a manual for such a thing, I have never seen it. Part of me was excited to see him because of all the wonderful times we had together in Tampa. Part of me was nervous about seeing him because Lee might be at home feeling like crap and imagining all kinds of illicit activities that would break his heart. Another part of me still kind of hated him because he might have contributed to the death of Autumn and because of how much pain Crys felt. I wasn't sure what I felt or what I should do, but when I saw him cross Eleventh Street and enter the meeting place exactly on time, I got out of the car, and followed suit.

I walked into the bar or coffee shop or both, and saw him standing at the long bar that made up the bulk of the left side of the room. An old Brandi Carlile song was coming through the speakers, as I surveyed my surroundings. Before the bar, there were seats along the left side of the wall with a stage and a pool table situated along the right side. Across from the bar, there were booths in a row occupying most of the right side of the wall, which was glass windows taller than me, until they stopped in front of a door that led out onto Eleventh Street. He was talking to the bartender or barista, and I heard him order a fancy espresso drink. I chuckled at the little similarity to Lee captured in that order. I ordered a coffee, and we waited together in silence for a few moments. He looked nervous and scared like the first few times I saw him in Tampa.

After we got our drinks, he pointed to the side door and we stepped out onto the sidewalk on Eleventh. There were tables and chairs on the sidewalk, and we sat down at the final set of them. It took David a minute because he was one of those people who kept his phone in the back pocket of his jeans, and at first, he almost sat on it. I found this funny while noticing this one wasn't a tracfone. He lit a smoke and offered me one saying, "This is the only time other than my little trips that I get to have these. My wife is not a fan."

"There are a lot of things about you she is not a fan of Paul."

"You're quite right Marshall," he says and blows out a stream of smoke. I light the one he gave me, and just look at him for a moment. It almost feels like we're back in Ybor sitting in similar chairs outside the Bricks after a dinner at one of the cafes nearby.

"So, you've known who I was for a while now according to a mutual friend in Milledgeville, that doesn't seem fair to me."

Laughing and appearing to relax a little bit, he says, "So you've met Lisa I see." He takes a puff of his smoke, shrugs his shoulders, and says, "Yeah, I about fainted when I saw your picture on that book jacket. At first, I was sure my head was playing tricks on me, but then I looked you up when I got home and realized Marshall was just as fake as Paul."

"Why didn't you say anything?"

"I figured you had just as many reasons for your fiction as I did for mine. Hell, that's what the damn book was about after all."

"I thought the same thing after I figured out who you were. I gotta say, it was quite a shock to see you at the flea market that day."

"For me too, I mean, I knew that Crystal and Lee came back, they got back before I left for my trips, and I knew they had another spouse because some of the people at the church were not happy about it, but I would have never guessed it was you. My wife mentioned you when I got home, but she didn't say a name and I didn't think to ask. I'm not even sure if she connected you to your books or not. It was odd. It is even funnier though, for me at least, because Lee was the old relationship I told you about that led me to try out Tampa in the first place. I went there thinking that maybe I would just get to see him one more time, but I never ran into him."

"Nope, you found his husband instead."

"I know, what are the odds," he says chuckling. He doesn't seem so nervous now, and I'm surprised at how easy it is to pick up our conversation pattern again after all that's happened. I guess a decade, even if only a few days a year, can't be erased overnight.

"So, David," I say his name slowly, "What are we doing here?"

"Well, I don't know how much you know about the town yet," he says starting to look and sound nervous again, "Or about my wife." He lights another cigarette, takes a sip of his coffee, looks around us like he often did in Tampa, and says, "I guess I'm wondering if I should be worried about having someone in town who knows what I do when I'm out of town." He tries to smile at me, but it comes out far too forced for me to buy it. He is scared I'm going to out him to the town, and I wonder if doing so would be fitting considering what happened to his sister. Luckily for him, I don't believe in outing people except in cases where they are targeting people like me politically or otherwise and must be stopped.

"You don't have anything to worry about in that regard. No one will learn about you, or us for that matter, from me. You start going after people like us like your flock," I say pointing back and forth between the two of us, "And that might change, but otherwise, your secret is safe with me." I can see the stress fall from his body as I speak. I wonder what it would be like to live in a place as small as Queens while always hoping – or maybe praying in his case – no one ever actually knows you.

"Thank you," he says in what reminds me of terrified whispers from victims on police procedural television shows.

"You should know, however, that Lee and Crystal now know about you because of our activities down in Tampa."

"Crystal can't be happy about that," he says, "I mean, about the two of us."

"Nope, not at all, and you should know that there is no 'us' anymore, and there won't be unless Crystal's opinion changes." I think about telling him about Lee's feelings too, but decide that is not my place. Even if Crys' opinion changed, I still wouldn't do anything without Lee's approval, and while that seems sad sitting here so close to a body and mind I've enjoyed so much, there is no doubt in my mind it is the best decision I can make for my life.

"I can't say I'm not disappointed, but that's kind of what I expected," he says putting out his cigarette and lighting another one. "Does Lee hate me too," he asks in that same scared whisper, and I realize he still has feelings for Lee. I'm not sure if I should tell Lee or not, but I think I should give those options some thought.

"No, Lee does not hate you," I say and watch his face brighten. "I don't think Lee ever did hate you to be honest."

"I always wondered, and I even thought about reaching out to him many times over the years, but I just never did. I guess I've never been the best at taking those kinds of risks in my life, and sometimes I wonder how my life would have been different if I had."

"Speaking of your life, how did you end up married to someone who hates people like us? I mean, come on, that is probably the most surprising part of all this for me."

"Do you know about my sister?"

"Yes."

"After she died, I was a mess man, I mean really a mess. She was my best friend, and I was even closer to her than I was to Lee. My whole world just went dark. I hated my parents, and the way they used the Bible to terrorize her so I went to Bible College thinking I could do it a different way and because it meant I could afford to go away since they would pay for it. The first job I got after school was with a youth group in Milledgeville, and that's where I met Linda. She was volunteering with the group. In any case, my dad's health was getting bad, and the people at the church were talking about me taking over, but they didn't want a single pastor. I wasn't out, never had been, but I had no interest in girls that I remember. At the same time, I thought I could do a lot of good at the church. Linda wanted out of her house, and she liked me. We were kind of dating at the camp, and I was the perfect Christian boyfriend because I had literally no interest in sex, well, at least sex with women."

He stirs his drink for a few seconds, sighs, and continues, "I don't really remember how it happened, but we were talking about the church and I said, I think I might have been joking honestly, maybe we should get married and run the church. I was surprised when she jumped at the idea, and I spent the whole engagement planning to run away, but again I just didn't. There are so many things I almost did that I didn't do, and the older I get the more that bothers me. But the next thing I knew, I was married and the pastor of dad's church. I don't know really, it kind of just happened."

He looks so sad, and I can't help but feel for him. At the same time, my curiosity is whispering in my ear. "How does that work if you have no interest in her, uh, physically?"

"Basically, like a friendship. We had sex occasionally when we were first together, but it's been years since then. Once we were married, I thought I should try, but it was just nothing and I don't think she liked being with me that way either honestly. We are basically friends who spend a lot of time apart. She has her books, which are often quite erotic, and that seems to be enough for her. I have my trips to Tampa between the two missionary trips I take each year, and you

179

know about those. We just don't talk about it. We live together, and we work together, but that's really about it."

"So, does she know about you, about your little trips?"

"Oh no, she would kill me," he says laughing and leaning back in his chair. "No, I'm laughing, but I think she might actually kill me if she found out. She thinks even the stuff in her books is a sin worthy of eternal damnation, and prays about the fact that she likes reading that stuff, including your books. No, she doesn't know, and I don't think she would react well if she did. She's been adamantly against sex in general the whole time I've known her, and it's only gotten worse in recent years with her and her friends buying into all the hate speech about people like you and me. I used to wonder if she suspected, but then it came up one night at a friend's house and her head almost exploded. Even the thought of it made her angry beyond words so I'm pretty sure she has no clue."

"Wow," I say, "That sounds so strange to me, I mean, my spouses know damn near everything I do, but yours doesn't even really know you at all it seems."

"It's a delicate balance, but not one I recommend," he says smiling. I try to imagine what it would be like to spend my life with someone who didn't know about a major part of who I am, but I draw a blank. Just like with the town, I can't conceptualize it, it makes no sense to me at all. I imagine it must feel very lonely. I imagine it must be difficult for all parties even if they don't realize it at the time. I imagine it is probably far more common than most people would like to admit. I can't imagine doing it myself.

"You ever think about just coming out, and seeing what happens?"

"Every day, every single day." He wipes his mouth and lights another smoke. He looks around us again, and I wonder how much time and energy it takes to stay hidden throughout a whole life. After a few minutes, he asks me about my impressions of the town, and we spend the next hour or so, after getting refills for our drinks, chatting about the town, reliving old times down in Tampa, working out ways he can help May from his position, and saying goodbye to our time as unknown lovers.

CHAPTER 26

A month after meeting with David, I have been summoned to Ruby's house. I arrive around lunchtime, and find her in her usual spot on the front porch swing. She is sipping sweet tea, and swinging back and forth as I arrive. She smiles at me, and motions to the empty space on the swing. I sit down, and ask, "You wanted to see me?"

I spent the morning on the phone with Lisa in Milledgeville discussing the details for some packages I wanted shipped down to the Tampa house for safe-keeping. The idea arose the day after I met up with David when Crys and I were looking for ways to consolidate things in the two houses. At the same time, Lisa came to town to purchase our second car for the whopping price of one dollar, and we figured she could help with the process. The whole time we had been in Queens one of our cars simply sat without use or need, and we finally decided to get rid of it when the right need arose. Lisa caught a ride to town with a friend headed to a concert in Augusta, and sat on our back porch after completing the sale.

"You realize y'all are a bunch of saints for basically giving this thing away," she asked sipping a coffee from Lee's new fancy espresso machine. The car is a mid-2000's Toyota sedan in perfect condition without all that many miles on it. When we lived in Tampa, Crys used it to get to work at USF, and Lee used the Honda to get to his office. Since I worked from home, I never needed a car during these times so we only had the two, and I would take one or the other – usually the Honda – out on the weekends. Since coming to Queens, we had even less use for a second car since we all basically worked from home or within two blocks of the house.

"We think it's the perfect use for the thing, and much better than it just sitting here taking up space," Crystal said with a smile. "We were also hoping you could help us out with something else today and in the coming weeks."

"Sure, what do you need," Lisa asked taking a sip of her drink and giving Lee a thumbs up that made him grin.

"I'm going to want to consolidate some books for storage in Tampa, and I thought it might be easier to do through your shop," I said smiling. "I have a couple packages for you to take today, and you can make sure they get to Tampa. Then, I'll send you the ones I already have, and orders for the other ones, and we'll just want you to make sure they get to Tampa safely so our neighbor can put them up in the house. It shouldn't take you too much time, and we're happy to pay for the time it does take."

"Don't worry about the time," Lisa says smiling at the first package Lee brings out of the house, "It sounds like fun and I'm sure it won't be much trouble." Lisa called while I was riding my bike over to Ruby's house to let me know everything would be in Tampa soon. I stood there, bike between my legs, and chatted with her for a few minutes. The car was working out perfectly, the shipments were no trouble, and everything seemed to be sailing along smoothly. I thanked her, and promised to come see her for coffee soon.

Ruby takes a sip of her tea, and says, "I wanted to talk to you about our little friend May." Her granddaughter came out, and asked if I wanted a drink, but I showed her my bottle of water and said no thanks. She stayed out for a few minutes, and we all talked about how well the kids were doing while they visited their own grandmother in Atlanta. After she went back inside, Ruby said, "I'm worried about that kid, their mama is on a rampage."

Ruby was right. Word was out all over town that the church ladies had found their new cause, and that Barb was leading the way. David tipped me off before they protested Chuck's. "Yeah, they were over at the shop a few days ago with hand painted signs about the dangers of bathrooms. We're hoping it will blow over."

"It might not," Ruby says with a concerned look on her face. "Nobody has seen or heard from May in weeks now, and it's got a lot of folk in town worried. People seem to be saying that either they sent May off somewhere or that little genius figured out a way to get out of here. I hope they got out of here, maybe went out on some river for some adventures and freedom. That's a happy thought," she says and I nod. "Either way, I don't know if this one is just going to blow over anytime soon."

182

As usual, Ruby was probably right. May was nowhere to be found, and people were looking for and asking about them all over town. The last time I saw May was the day they turned up at the diner, right after I got back from Augusta, with bruises covering various parts of their body. May was scared, and worried that their parents were going to do something even more drastic. Lee helped May get cleaned up, get some food, and consider the options they had in front of them. No one had seen May since that night, and rumors were flying all over town. Some people were certain that May had run off with a group of hippies out of Athens to pursue a music career. Others were just as sure May had gone ahead over to Augusta to get an early start on college classes since they didn't need to stick around for the graduation ceremony later in the year. Others were saying they'd seen a strange man hanging around town, and maybe he had abducted our poor little May right out of their bedroom one night.

The rest of the town was sure it had to do with Barb showing up at Chuck's with her friends and screaming at Crystal and Lee. Some folks thought maybe Crystal was having an affair with May that had gone wrong. Other folks had learned about the transgender element of Barb's anger, through the protest or the rumor mill, and thought that either the sick girl had been sent to doctors for her own good or the poor child had been unfairly sent away by stupid bigots depending on their political perspective. Some people blamed the church, and lit up its phone lines. Other people blamed my family, and the already reduced business at the diner dropped off even more. Opinions and information on the situation were split in a variety of ways throughout the town, but nobody was talking about anything else and everyone was sure they knew what happened.

"I hope you're wrong this time, but you might be right," I say staring out into the grass where a group of kids have started playing. A couple of them wave to Ruby – and maybe to me as well – and we wave back.

"Well, you just be careful, you hear, people are awfully mad, and I know you and your family were planning to stay here, but you might not be able to after this."

"I appreciate the heads up Ruby, how are you doing with all this?"

"Me, oh sugar, I'm what they call bulletproof in this town. Ain't nobody going to give me no hard time associating with y'all, or for helping that kid. A couple people have made some not very nice phone calls, thinking I have something to do with this the same way they think I know everything, you see, but that don't bother me none. I just want to make sure our little May is safe and sound, same as always, so I'm not worried about no stupid folks. You just be careful and watch out for your family, and I'll take care of mine the same." With that, Ruby pats me on the back, and says, "Don't you need to be getting on over to our other friends," and I laugh wondering once again if this lady really does know everything.

I leave Ruby's house and ride my bike down to the café on Main Street beside the library. When I arrive, I see Lacey, Kate, and Sylus already sitting outside waiting on me. We agreed to meet for lunch the day before so we could catch up on all the events in town. I know each of them are worried about May after years of watching over them, but I also know there isn't anything I can tell them that they don't already know. I'm reminded of one of Lee's favorite phrases – "We'll know what we know when we know it." It's not much, but it somehow comforts me as I lock up my bike on the rack in front of the library.

As I sit down at the table, Sylus asks, "Any word from May?" The others stare at me with obvious anticipation and worry. I wish I had something to tell them.

"Nope, no word at all yet. I'm hoping that means May is fine, but I have no way to know that right now." I wish I had more to say as I watch their faces drop in unison. Like Ruby and my family, these people have been outlets and safe spaces for May, and they feel invested in what happens. Somewhere in a shop nearby, I hear a k.d. lang song playing faintly, and I remember that Crystal said that was Autumn's favorite singer. I push thoughts of Autumn out of my head, and try to focus on the conversation at hand.

"Is there anything we can do," Lacey asks sipping her water and looking at me with wide eyes. It's the same question she asked yesterday, and I know she knows that too. Sometimes waiting is the hardest part.

"Not yet, we just have to wait until we hear from May. Until then, there is nothing we can do except hope they are okay and be ready to help out if needed."

"It seems like only yesterday May and Samantha practically lived in the library looking through books, drawing future lives, and laughing without a care in the world. I think I might give anything to go back to those days knowing everything we do now. I feel like I could have done something more to help back then," Kate says as our food arrives. "The two of them, even a few days ago, were always so cute together, but Samantha is certain May is fine."

We spend the meal talking about memories of May, concerns about May's mother, and plans for what to do if things go bad in town. We imagine May on some interstate highway with their hair flowing in the breeze, an Against Me record blaring from the stereo, and freedom at the tip of their fingers. We imagine May with another name and a transformed body imparting their wisdom to students or politicians or some other audience years from now, and discuss the ways their rapid-fire brain could impact the world. We imagine a lot of things we hope we will get to see, and leave out the things we wish not to see. We laugh about May dancing with wild abandon in the record store, holding a pretend wedding with Samantha in the library a couple years ago just for fun, and showing up barraging us with an endless series of questions and theories about the world.

After the meal, I ride my bike over to the cemetery and sit by Autumn's grave for a little while. It's quiet and peaceful in this spot, and it looks like Crys was here recently because a fresh tulip is keeping me company. I remember how May looked the last time I saw them. Their face contained a mixture of fear and determination, and they seemed to carry a confidence and strength that was missing the first time I met them. I remembered they gave me a slip of paper from their journal, and said they wanted me to keep it safe. I pulled the sheet of paper out of my pocket sitting there beside Autumn's final resting place, and read it to myself again. It was just one word, just a name, but I hoped to say it to May one day.

"You doing okay Jacks," Crystal said walking up to where I was sitting. "I thought I might find you out here when you didn't show up at the diner with Lacey and the others after dinner." It had become almost a standard ritual that we all went for coffee, and maybe just one little piece of pie, after each time the four of us met for dinner downtown. I didn't feel like it that day. I just wanted to go somewhere quiet and think about May. "Is that May's chosen name," she asked looking at the piece of paper in my hands.

"Yes," I said softly handing the sheet of paper to her. May told her they were thinking about names because their birth name didn't feel right one day in the office. Crystal showed May a place online where people talked about how they chose their names, and the reasons for such choices. She then walked May through the steps it would take to change a dead name in Georgia and in Florida in case May decided to do so. It felt like this event took place both so long ago and within a few minutes.

Crystal looked at the piece of paper, smiled at me, and said, "I think it fits May pretty well, and I think it shows that no matter what happens, you did the right thing by being there for them in every way you could."

CHAPTER 27

It wasn't the first time. There was the time in the late-sixties when racial tensions overflowed, just prior to the Augusta riots, because of two young people of different colors who ran off together. There was the time in the seventies when protests by women in the factories near the town led to tension in the streets. There was the time in the eighties fights and tensions within the school boiled over until the lightning storm brought the town together. There was the time in the nineties when the first group of kids sought to create a gay-straight alliance at the high school a few years before Crystal and Lee went there. It wasn't the first time, but it still felt damn ominous to us.

We were awoken just before five that morning by the call from the police. We had fallen asleep together the night before after staying up late on Face time chats with a friend in Florida. Lee answered the phone as Crys and I made unrecognizable noises, but all hopes of going back to sleep vanished when he shouted, "WHAT," and rolled out of bed to frantically end the call and start putting on clothes. Both Crys and I were startled to hear Lee's exclamation, and immediately asked what was happening. The two of us followed suit as Lee filled us in, and a few minutes later the three of us walked up to Chuck's.

We saw the damage the moment we turned the corner. There was toilet paper everywhere, trash strewn throughout the parking lot, and it looked like a collection of beer cans in the far corner of the lot. Familiar words were spray painted on some of the walls and windows. There was the rendering of "Go Home Faggots" in orange on the window spanning the bottom of the T, and the bright red "Tranny Lovers" written on the glass of the entrance. There were a few other colorful slurs here and there, but the message was the same. The police admitted right away that there was likely no way to find out who did it, and we admitted among ourselves that we needed to have a conversation about our future in Queens.

After the police left, we began cleaning up the place with the help of regulars and our employees – including those who were supposed to be off that day. We didn't serve much food, and only allowed employees and regulars into the restaurant. The paper sent someone out to take a photo, and I wondered if a future version of me would see the photo twenty years from now when his father in law fucked with his life. I cursed Chuck a little more than usual, and I think even Crystal and Lee did the same. By the middle of the afternoon, we had almost everything cleaned up, and all the writing on the windows removed or at least obscured. We agreed that we needed to have a chat, and decided to do so after closing that night.

Around 2 p.m., we officially re-opened the place for limited food and beverages because Lee did not want the perpetrators to feel like they knocked us down for even a day. Despite the chaos outside, the inside had been left untouched, and we took this as a piece of good news. Throughout the afternoon, a few of the regulars held court at the bar, and people from all over town came by wishing us well and talking about what a shame it was. We took turns going back home to clean up from the earlier clean up, and by around four in the afternoon Crys was holding court in the office, Lee was running the grill and chatting people up like any other day, and I grabbed my usual spot at the bar with the regulars.

"Any word from little May," Richard asked as I sat down. No one had heard from May in just over four months at this point, and their disappearance was still the talk of the town. If anything, the recognition of the town, about six weeks after May disappeared, that even their mom had no clue where they were only enhanced the gossip. Barb went with the police on a house to house search for May, and no one was surprised which house was first on the list even though more than a few people seemed shocked that we didn't have May hidden in our basement, attic, or some other crawl space.

"Honestly, the fact that Barb did not send the kid away tells me none of us are likely to ever see May again," I said lighting the smoke Lee said was allowed inside on this day. For my part, I was correct. I never did see May again.

Doris tapped her spoon on her coffee cup, and said, "It is such a shame, I mean, she was such a sweet girl, so smart too, and her mama basically ran her off for being different."

"Yeah, but it happens all the time," Tim said chewing on his dip. "People just have trouble dealing with new things, don't know why, just seems that way."

"You think maybe she'll go somewhere and become a boy y'all," asked Matt.

"I don't know how she could," Richard says. "Think about it, young kid, no real money, no real transportation, only a high school education – this isn't the sixties anymore. She'll probably be out on the street or waiting tables somewhere would be my guess. I mean, I heard them hormone things and surgeries are kind of expensive even with Obamacare." Richard pounds his hand on the table as if that's the end of the matter, and everyone chuckles a bit.

"I don't know about that Richard," Doris says, "She could have gotten some help before she left town." She glances in my direction, and says, "And didn't y'all say she got into college down in Florida or something."

"Yeah, they did get into college, but they'll still need money to go," I say.

"Maybe those ladies at the record store and the library helped her out, they was always looking after her, so was ole Sylus, maybe they gave her some money," Matt says. "Or, maybe she'll join the military and get money that way, it could happen."

"I doubt it," Richard says and takes another sip from his cup. "If May was going to go that route, she would be here living with Jackson and his weird family, we all know that." Everyone chuckles, glances at me, and looks away just as quickly. I'm aware that, like the rest of the town, they think I know something about what happened to May.

"You know what I think," Shelby says while refilling Darryl's cup. "I bet Miss Ruby helped him get out of here. Think about it, even she says she don't know where May is, but Miss Ruby hears everything and we all know that. With May, though, all she'll say is her money is on the river, and chuckle. She knows something. There's a river in Augusta not far from the college and that there gay church, that's probably it. Ruby was in on it, I'm sure, I just bet she's behind it somehow."

Richard looks up and says, "I don't know about the Augusta part, Ruby is always saying stuff like 'love the woods' or 'watch the sky,' but her being involved in this, yes, now that might be possible, I mean, didn't her kid become some kind of fancy lawyer up in Atlanta? They got money, Ruby and them, and little May did used to always go out there and talk to Ruby and borrow her black books."

"Black books," I ask.

"You know what I mean," Richard says, "Them novels written by black women about life down here back when, like the one they made a movie of that ole Oprah was in."

Doris adds, "I bet it was Miss Ruby. She is always working on things and always knows things, how else could she not know where May got to."

"Y'all are missing the obvious, yep, you are," Tim says, "What if her mama did send her off to one of those facilities, but just don't want nobody to know? Think about it, her mama thinks people like May are sick, and that would be embarrassing to the family. She could have just quietly shipped her off, and just be putting on a show for the rest of us until May comes back, yep, that could be it."

I enjoyed all the speculation, and I noticed that none of them seemed to mention the top theory in town while they were at Chuck's. Ruby even confirmed that most of the people in town still thought we were hiding May somewhere nearby. We were not, but that was the top theory circulating, and the one Barb still seemed to be invested in as she drove by our house every night far too slowly for comfort. On the bright side, I was now on a first name basis with all the police officers in town, and each one had complimented my home on at least one of the occasions it was searched. Not exactly the form of integration into the town I was looking for, but entertaining for me nonetheless. I remember wondering if people would still be sitting here debating this topic years later, and something told me that was an incredibly likely outcome. When the conversation finally ran its course, they all got quiet for a few minutes, just like they always did, until the next thread emerged.

"What are y'all going to do Jackson," Darryl asked pointing out toward the parking lot.

"I don't know, we'll have to figure that out as a family," I say looking at Lee. Lee didn't say anything, but we both knew the decision would ultimately be up to Crys because we weren't going anywhere without her, and this was her family's creation.

"Do you think they'll do anything worse," Doris asked looking genuinely concerned, but whether for us or her favorite hang out I couldn't tell.

"I don't think so," I said, not sure if I believed the words myself, "But we'll keep an eye out and do what we can to be safe just in case. I'm hoping it was just some stupid teenagers getting their rocks off, and that we've seen the worst of it." I caught Lee's eye as I spoke, and thought about all the phone calls where people just hung up over the last few months. He was starting to get a little scared, and Crys and I were too. At the same time, Crys made it clear, even today, that she didn't want to let go of this place while it survived, and we figured that meant we were still here for the long haul until we heard otherwise from the boss.

Around 8 p.m., about an hour before closing time for the night, the place became deserted, and Lee sent Shelby home. Crys and I were sitting at the bar looking over the police report, and the numbers for the restaurant. Lee came over to where we were sitting, took a cigarette from the latest pack I wasn't supposed to have, and lit it. He stood there behind the bar silently for a couple minutes, and then asked, "So, what are we going to do?"

"Crys," I said looking at her and lighting my own cigarette.

"For now," she said slowly and softly, "We stay unless one or both of you really needs to leave." Sighing, she added, "In that case, you should go and I'll stay at least for now."

"I'm not leaving without you," I say, and Lee nods emphatically.

"Then, for now at least, we stay," she says, "But I think we should start getting things ready in case we need to leave." She lights her own cigarette, and says, "I don't want to give up this place if I don't have to, but I also won't risk our family." She takes a deep breath, lets it out, takes a puff of her smoke, lets it out, and says, "I honestly think it was just a few teenagers or maybe older kids who did this, and that it's not a real threat. Even if I'm wrong, vandalism, phone calls and dirty looks are a few steps from serious violence for me. I understand if y'all feel differently, but for me, we're not done here yet."

"And if it gets worse," Lee asks tapping ashes from his cigarette.

"If it gets worse, we get out of here and never come back. Our family still comes first."

"Jacks," Lee says, and they both turn to me.

"In many ways, I think we all know this is my fault." They both start to protest, but I motion for them to stop. "Look, I'm not saying I did anything wrong here, but I did choose to take May under my wing and I did refuse to stand by when their mom wanted to make them feel worthless and when they showed up with bruises. I understand that y'all were with me every step of the way, and I love you both for that, but I set these events in motion, and I'm just saying I'm aware of that fact as I speak to you two right now."

They both slowly nod. We all knew that May was the straw that broke the towns back in relation to our family, and we all know that happened because I chose to be there for May in the first place. They might not have liked us before, but the town tolerated us quietly and without phone calls or vandalism. We all also knew that I was the one who never wanted to come here in the first place, and that I was the one who brought the pastor into our family accidentally after what happened almost twenty years before. For whatever reason, I wanted these things to be clear to them and right out in the open before I shared my opinion that night.

"I think we all also know that I didn't want to come here, and that my history with David caused us all strife as well." They again start to speak, and I again motion for quiet. "I want y'all to think about all these things because my honest opinion is that we should stay here until the moment comes that we are all ready to go. As long as either of you want to be here, or need to be here, I will stay and I don't care about the risks because you two are all that really matters as far as I'm concerned. So, if Crys wants to stay, I say we stay."

I watch both their faces register surprise followed by concern followed by joy, and then Lee says, "Then we stay," and all of us nod. With that, the three of us begin cleaning up the inside of the restaurant so it will be ready for the next day. Lee takes the kitchen, Crys takes the top of the T, and I take the bottom of the T. As closing time draws near, we crank up Pearl Jam on the jukebox, and dance our way to a clean restaurant. The clock reads 8:58 p.m. when we each hear the bell on the front door go off for the last time that night. I turn toward the door, and there is David standing in the entryway.

CHAPTER 28

"What the fuck are you doing here," Crys yells across the room, and David flinches as if he's been shot. I get the distinct impression that the look on his face means he is rethinking coming here tonight and wondering if he'll make it home. Lee and I both move quickly to get between them just in case a brawl is about to break out, and the guitar solo coming from the jukebox feels somewhat appropriate. Lee comes around the counter to where Crys is, and I move up the bottom of the T to position myself directly in between the two of them. I have no clue what David is doing here, but this might be the last place and the last day he should have showed up.

If there was one moment where my hatred for Chuck reached its zenith, this was that moment. I remember wishing we had never come here, and wondering what the hell we had gotten ourselves into. I honestly could not think of anything worse after the day we just had than David walking into a showdown with Crys. Where was Chuck when I needed someone to punch, I thought and braced myself for the carnage I was sure I was about to watch. Lee looked terrified, Crys looked ready to pounce, and David looked like a rat caught in a trap.

"I came to apologize for the vandalism on behalf of the town, and to see if there was anything I could do." Even I can hear the fear and hesitancy in his voice as he speaks.

"A little late aren't you buddy," I say standing in between the two of them as Lee puts his arm around Crystal only to have it shaken off by her the next moment. Lee is obviously not thinking. Crys is twice as strong as either of us, and he knows he won't be able to stop her if she goes after David. Hell, she'll probably run through me like a bulldozer. I'm taking another approach. I'm trying to break the tension, do something funny, anything to keep this situation from becoming the nightmare I have playing in my head.

"I was over in Augusta all day, and just found out about it when I got back into town," he says, his voice shaking a bit. At least he's smart enough to be afraid of Crys. "I also wanted to make sure y'all were alright," he says looking directly at Lee.

Lee and David have been trading messages for months now. After we met in Augusta, I told Lee that I thought David still had feelings for him, and he became curious. The three of us talked about it over the course of three nights, and though Crys did not like it, she agreed that Lee should figure out how he felt and what he needed for himself. Her only request was that Lee kept us informed of anything that happened, and kept David away from her. This arrangement seemed to be working out rather well until now. Crystal looks ready for blood, and David looks like he wants to run away. Lee just looks about as confused and concerned as I feel standing in the middle of a long brewing confrontation.

"We're fine, now get out," Crys says still approximating a yell, but not quite as loud as earlier, "You have no right to be here." She looks ready for a fight, and I of all people know that look all too well, David needs to get out of here as fast as he can, I think.

You see, at this point, the smart money would suggest that David should call this a win, I mean, he did walk in here and speak without bodily harm so that's a win in this case, and get the hell out of here before anything gets worse. If he is as smart as he seems, I think, that's exactly what he will do. Hoping to help this decision-making process, I say, "Yeah, we're okay man, you should probably head on home. We've had a long day, and just need some time to process everything as a family." I see Lee nodding, and David takes a step as if to turn around and leave. Yes, I think, this will be the end of it, at least for now. Come on, David, take the way out she just handed you, and let us get back to our uneasy equilibrium. You can do it, I have faith in you, walk through the door and call Lee later.

He doesn't do this. Instead, he turns around after first turning toward the door, and says, "Are you ever going to get over this stuff Crystal?"

For what seems like an eternity or maybe even longer, you could hear a pin drop in the restaurant. I'm stunned. Lee looks stunned. Crystal looks stunned. David looks more stunned than all of us put together. Did he just say that? Did he just say that to Crystal of all the people on the planet? Are we about to finally watch Crys murder someone after all the jokes about it over the years? What the hell is he thinking, he can't be this damn stupid! The air in the restaurant feels heavier somehow. Everything is moving in slow motion, and it is so quiet. If I'm being honest with you, I am more than a little bit terrified of whatever is coming next. At the same time, I'm somehow frozen in place, incapable of even the slightest movement, as I watch Crys break away from Lee, move past me with the speed of a cheetah or an Olympian or maybe even something more ferocious than that, and launch herself into David on the opposite side of the room from where she had been standing a few seconds ago.

"CRYS," Lee yells from the other side of the top of the T where he also appears glued to the floor. We both just stand by helpless watching the conflict unfold.

As Crys collides into David his body slams against the door, and she begins pounding on his chest, swinging her arms as hard as she can, and screaming, "YOU FUCKING KILLED HER YOU FUCKING ASSHOLE YOU FUCKING KILLED HER," over and over again. There are almost two decades worth of tears embedded within each punch, and Crystal is letting them all out tonight in one fell swoop. All her anger, all her grief, all the memories her and Autumn did not get to make supplement each swing.

David doesn't fight back at all. He just stands there, and then goes down on one knee as Crys continues beating on him with all her might screaming, crying, and shaking. The sound of the repeated blows fills my head, far louder than they should be. Finally, I move again, and so does Lee. We both run toward the two of them as fast as we can, and pull Crys, kicking and still screaming, off David as he falls to the floor. In the morning, we'll realize that we each got a couple bruises in the process, but we don't notice at the time. At the time, all that matters is that our wife has finally unleashed all her feelings about Autumn's death and we need to find a way to protect her and David from both David and herself. We hold Crys together in our four arms, and her screams start to fade into whispers of the same phrase as her body is wracked by sobs.

In the end, we're all on the floor of the top of the T. David is over by the door holding his chest, struggling a little bit for breath, and crying silently. Crys, Lee, and I are wrapped up together a few feet away. Crys is dry heaving and shaking as tears continue to pour down her face. Lee is crying and cursing while rubbing a leg he apparently injured in the melee. I feel tears running down my own face, a dull ache growing on my chest, and a growing numbness in the arm that is inconveniently located under Crys and Lee. The four of us lay there in our own messed up positions for a few minutes as the town goes on about its peaceful, quiet business outside the restaurant. I think we're all hoping it's over.

That is, until, David opens his damn mouth again. For me, it feels like he is trying to steal my hatred from Chuck. "I didn't kill my sister," he says softly, almost a whisper, and starts to sit up. The three of us were already starting to get up as well, and he repeats the statement a little louder, "I didn't kill my sister."

From her position kneeling on the floor, Crys says, "You might as well have when you told your parents about us," in her own version of a tired whisper.

"I didn't tell my parents anything Crystal," he says. Then, in a louder and angrier voice, he says, "I didn't tell them anything, they found out and punished us both!"

"It had to be you," Crys says in the same angry tone, but her voice starts shaking, maybe something in his voice gave her pause, and she says, "No one else knew about us." I remember her saying these same words in the cemetery, but this time she doesn't sound as sure of herself. She sounds like she's just repeating the phrase without the same confidence she had in the cemetery when she told me the details surrounding Autumn's death. I can somehow feel her grief in the air, it covers everything in the restaurant.

Lee and I are both sitting on our tired butts watching. I look at him. He looks at me. We both shrug. Crys is crouching as if she is planning another assault, but David has sat back down and is leaning against the wall wiping tears from his face. In a voice that is barely audible and between his own throaty sobs, he says, "They, uh, they over, they…" before starting to cry about as hard as Crys was earlier.

Crys stares a hole through him, starts shaking her head from side to side, and sits down on her legs holding her head in her hands. "They," David tries again, "They overheard us when we got home that night Crystal, I didn't tell them about any of us and I never would have, I can't believe you thought that," and begins crying harder as Crys sits on the floor between Lee and I shaking.

All of us sit there quietly for a few minutes. David's words hang in the air like some kind of fog, and he and Crystal continue crying. He looks just as tortured as she does, and they both seem completely out of it. I look at Lee, and he mouths 'Holy Shit' and I mouth back 'I know'. We both watch the other two, and then I get up and go get us both cigarettes we are not supposed to have. We stand behind where Crys is seated on the floor, closer to where we had our family discussion earlier, and smoke waiting to see what they will say or do next. Later, we agree that it was like we had no words, no way to express what we felt, and no way to imagine what the two of them must have been going through. We were just tired.

At some point, time is hard to capture in such moments, Crys said, "What happened," in what may have been the most pained and frightened tone I have ever heard.

Taking a long, deep breath, David said, "We were coming back from the party, and we were outside talking like we always did. We didn't talk about me and Lee or you and her in the house just in case because you remember mama liked to eavesdrop on us. So, we were talking outside and I was telling her that I finally told Lee I loved him," Lee smiles big at this memory, which I had not yet heard, and I wonder why he never said anything. "And she told me she was in love with you, more than she had been before, and that y'all were finally getting close, you know, physically. We were celebrating Crys, you were queen, we were all in love, it was the best day of our lives," he says before choking on his sobs again.

"You knew about us," Crys says and beside me Lee looks confused as he nods as if to say, 'duh, I knew that.'

"Of course I did, she was my sister Crys! Why do you think you were always invited everywhere we went? I knew about you two from the day you first kissed her in the back of this building, when you got so nervous you kept stuttering before and after the kiss. She came home happier than I had ever seen her that day, and told me all about it. I even know you gave her a tulip from Miss Ruby's garden the next day when you were worried you shouldn't have kissed her and she kissed you on the nose and told you how she felt!" We all knew the story of Crys' first kiss, though I didn't know until that moment that Autumn was the kiss because Crys had never mentioned who the person was when she told the story. I also realized later that neither Lee nor I had known the rest of the story, the true origin of the tulips between them.

Her face fell, she let out a loud wail, and said again, "What happened," in the same tired, tear-soaked voice.

"Mom heard a noise outside right before we got there, and Dad was on the side of the house checking it out," he takes a deep breath, "We didn't see him, we didn't know he was there. He heard the whole conversation and later that night he beat us both and lectured us on his version of Christian virtue. He was so angry, he said the devil had stolen his children, and he just lost it and kept going after us for months after that. Nothing we did was good enough after that night, and our house became like a prison or something, but Autumn, oh my god," his voice cracks, "She got it even worse than I did." David starts crying again, and Crys looks like she might faint. David breathes in and out like he is doing those breathing strategies they teach people in preparation for having a baby. He keeps doing this for a while before speaking again. Finally, he says, "I couldn't stop it, I tried, but I couldn't stop it, I'm so sorry I couldn't stop it, I'm so sorry," and devolves into another fit of sobs on the floor.

"Why didn't you tell me," Crys finally screams at him after a few minutes of silence.

"I thought you knew all this, I thought Autumn put it in the letter I mailed you! I blamed myself for not being able to save her, and I just thought you did too and that's why you hated me. That's why I HATE ME! That's why I didn't try to follow you and Lee when you left."

"You knew about the letter," Crys says and falls into a crouch punching the floor.

"I sent you the letter, I remember putting the tulip stamp you gave her on the envelope so you would be sure to open it right away. I just didn't know what was in it, and when I got back home from my church work punishment that night, she was gone. I've spent my life wishing I opened that letter and found a way to save her!"

Lee and I are still at the bar during this whole exchange, but neither of us knows what, if anything, we can possibly say. Crys has spent the better part of two decades blaming David for Autumn's death, David has spent the better part of two decades blaming himself for this death and thinking Crys had every right to hate him, and Lee lost his first love based on this information. We just stood there in shock, watching these two revise what we thought we knew, and trying to wrap our heads around it. Lee started crying at some point, and I put my arms around him and held him close. There was nothing else to do. There was nothing I could say. I watched my wife, my husband and my former favorite as they relived the worst moments of their lives.

CHAPTER 29

I finally stopped hating Chuck two weeks later as Lee and I looked at magazines at the Barnes & Noble in Ocala, Florida. Crystal was searching for something new to listen to on the rest of our drive. By my estimate, we were now at least five hours from Queens, and more importantly, we were very unlikely to ever visit that place again. Our home was an hour and a half south, and I couldn't wait to sit on my old porch, crack jokes with Marcus, and forget the past year. I didn't plan or expect it, but suddenly I realized I simply was not angry with Chuck anymore. In some ways, I felt like Chuck had, in a way, given me some pretty cool gifts I could have only gotten in Queens.

Our trip south began unexpectedly the night after David came to the diner when the lightning storms finally arrived. We were at home, huddled together on the couch we rarely ever seemed to use in the living room, still processing David's accidental coming out to the town, when we got the call from the police. Lee had been on the phone with David most of the day, and Crystal was still in shock after the events of the previous evening. I was taking care of them both when the phone rang, and I decided I would get up to see what was happening. I picked up the phone, and a voice I didn't recognize said, "Mr. Garner, uh, you might want to go up to the restaurant to see if there is anything you can save."

I relayed the message to Crystal and Lee, and we took the short walk that had become so common over the past year. When we turned the corner, Crys said, "Woah," and I just started laughing without being able to stop. Lee was silent as we stood there together watching the flames jump all over the restaurant, and felt the heat engulf the place. We stood there for about an hour watching it burn. The firewoman on the scene explained that one of the lightning bolts must have hit the transformer at the restaurant because the whole thing was beyond their help by the time they arrived about twenty minutes before I got the call. After the year we just experienced, there was something fitting about the sight of Chuck's – A Queen's Tradition burning to the ground before our very eyes.

The next morning, we were sitting on the back porch having cigarettes we weren't supposed to have and drinking coffee made by Lee's fancy machine. Crys got off the phone, and said, "It looks like the only options are to sell the property or to rebuild from scratch."

"Too much damage for repair," Lee asked.

"Way too much," Crys said.

"Well, what do we want to do," Lee asked looking at Crystal.

"I think it's your call Crys," I said lighting another smoke, and Lee nodded. "We have the money and the time so we can rebuild it ourselves if you want to." Lee and I both turned to look at Crystal, and she nodded at us. "So, what do you want to do?"

Smiling, she said, "It's time to go home, our real home."

"Really," I asked trying and failing to hide my excitement. I could feel the gulf breeze on my skin already.

"Are you sure," Lee asked also failing to hide his own growing desire to leave the place now that David was moving out of Queens and the restaurant was in ashes.

"Yeah, I'm sure," she said smiling at both of us. "We did what we came here to do. We kept the business going until it was done, we worked through all our old memories, and we honored mom and dad's dreams." She looked thoughtful for a moment, and then she continued, "Think about it y'all, everyone in town thinks we either were involved in May's disappearance, caused David to become gay, or both, and we all know this town has a long memory. I think we needed to come here, I really do, but now I think it's time to get back to our life."

There was no argument. We began packing almost immediately, and I handled shipping the things we wanted to keep down to Tampa. Lacey was interested in Chuck's old house, and we gave it to her for a steal on the condition that the sign would never be taken down while she was there. Her friend Cat was coming to stay for a while, and the two of them would use the house for years to come. Crystal handled the paperwork for the restaurant while I went with Lee to help David get his stuff from his former home and make plans for relocating to Atlanta or maybe Florida sometime soon. We said our goodbyes to

Kate, Ruby, Sylus, and the regulars from Chuck's, and spent some time with Lisa on our way out of town. We took photos of the three of us in front of the burned-out lot that once was Chuck's, and made sure to pose the same way we did when we took pictures in front of the place my first week in town. On our final night in Queens, we stood in the den staring at the sign and holding hands for a good thirty minutes. It was time to put the place to rest, and get ready for the adventure awaiting us down south.

I was sitting outside the Barnes & Noble sipping a Starbucks coffee thinking about everything that happened in our last weeks in Georgia. I smiled to myself, and even the thought of Chuck for a few minutes too. After purchasing his three sports magazines, and Crys' two new Counting Crows albums, Lee sat down in the chair beside me. A few minutes later, Crys joined us under the little covering on the porch, and said, "Y'all ready to go home?"

"Jacks has been ready for about a year now, I think," Lee said poking me in the shoulder. "I think it's the right thing, and it will be nice to be back. Hell, maybe I'll finally write my book this year, what do you think?"

"I'm sure you will," I say and all three of us laugh. "How are you feeling about leaving Queens Crys?" I reach out and take her hand in the one of mine Lee isn't holding, and she smiles at me in that special way only people who have been through tough stuff together over time seem to be able to do.

"I feel good Jacks, I feel good." She blows on her iced coffee, takes her hand back, and offers each of us one of the three remaining cigarettes we weren't supposed to have while we were in Georgia. We all light up, and Crys says, "I think there will always be a part of me buried up there with Autumn, with my parents, and I think it was important to revisit those streets and ghosts." Lee and I both nod, and she continues, "But that is not my home anymore, you two goofballs are and Tampa is," she pauses, pulls on her lip, and says, "And hell, I hope Alice is, well, if she'll give me another chance when we get back. Either way, I think I'm done being a former homecoming queen from Queens."

"What about you Lee? How are you feeling," I ask.

"I feel pretty good honestly," Lee says smiling, "I know David and I need to figure out what we feel for each other, but now that we know he didn't betray Autumn and Crys can talk about her feelings without hating him, I feel a kind of peace I never really expected to reach with our hometown." As he finished speaking, Crys and I both got up and hugged him. Smiling within our embrace, he said, "Right now, I just want to go home and see what's next."

That night in the diner, Crys and David reached a truce I never would have imagined. After they had shared it all, cried all the tears they had, and seen each other's pain, a calm descended on the restaurant. David apologized for her pain, and she apologized for his pain. Everything was not magically better all the sudden and we all admitted that it might never be, but the four of us found a peace agreement that we thought would allow us all to continue to heal, communicate, and understand each other in the future. Crys suggested Lee walk David out so they could spend a few minutes alone, and with a grin too big for words the two of them left the restaurant headed out in the direction of where David lived.

The next morning at home, we didn't talk about the night before, and we all kind of silently agreed that we needed a day off from emotions. Unfortunately, when we got to the restaurant that morning, the town had other plans. While we slept, David's wife had kicked him out of the house after meeting him in the doorway when he arrived. David had pocket dialed her about the same time Crystal slammed him into the wall that night, and she heard the whole conversation about Autumn, David, Lee, and Crystal. A pocket dial, one little moment, how often did one moment change a life? I thought about how funny I found it that he kept the phone in his back pocket that day in Augusta, and couldn't stop laughing for a while.

According to David, his wife sat there listening to the conversation growing angrier and angrier about the lies, the sexless marriage, and the feeling that she had been tricked. She went through his stuff, and found messages he traded with Lee via email in recent weeks. She stared at a picture of him standing in front of a Tampa church, and wondered what he really did down there where Lee lived all those years. She thought about his work with the gay churches, and wondered if he laughed at her when was out with 'those people.' David was out, and though a bit stunned, by the time he swung by our house the next night to see Lee, he was, as he said on the back porch when Crys asked how he was doing, "feeling surprisingly relieved despite how it happened." The story flowed like wine, and it seemed that everyone was certain that it was ultimately our fault.

As we left I-75 for the 275 stretch that ran through the Tampa Bay area, I wondered if Lee or I would spend more intimate time with David in the coming years. Lee had loved him for most of his life and I had spent a decade of short visits with him, but I had trouble imagining what might come next for the three of us. Maybe it was the fact that I was going home. Maybe it was the fact that I never wanted to leave Tampa in the first place. Maybe I was too excited about Tampa. Maybe I was just in shock after everything that had happened in the past year. I didn't know what it was. In that moment, my imagination failed me, and all I wanted to do was camp out on my porch in South Tampa and never leave.

"You okay Jacks," Crystal asked.

"Yeah, I was just thinking," I said from the backseat.

Lee turned around, and said, "Sure feels good to be home, doesn't it?"

Crys and I both said yes, and she took the exit for Howard and Armenia. We were back in the city, and I could already feel and hear the difference all around me. I wondered what the people in Queens were saying about us right now. I thought about the fun times I had with Sylus, Ruby, Lacey, Kate, May and Lisa. I imagined myself finding a new favorite next time I went to Ybor just in case things got serious with David and Lee, sitting on the porch trading insults with Marcus, and being fabulous with Alice while hoping she still wanted Crys now that Crys was ready to be serious with her. I also knew, after some lessons learned in Queens, I would have some new responsibilities when we got home. As we passed Kennedy Boulevard, I heard the familiar sound of sirens, and saw lights flashing somewhere to the left. Smiling, I thought, I'm home again.

We didn't unpack the car when we got home. It could wait a few hours or days. We went inside, and separated into our individual favorite spaces. Lee went to the kitchen, and started playing with his toys, turning knobs, and thinking out loud about his next dinner party. Crystal climbed up in her favorite bay window, pulled out one of her folders from her most recent research project, and began chewing a pencil while going over her notes. I grabbed the turntable I used outside, set it up on the porch, and started Pink Floyd's *Wish You Were Here*. I grabbed a Florida Cracker from the refrigerator, thank you Marcus I thought as I popped the top, and took my usual spot out on the porch with my own journal and thoughts.

After Pink Floyd finished, I put on an Against Me record and looked out at the street as a familiar Toyota pulled up to the curb. I sat my journal down, took a sip of my beer, and let out a satisfied sigh. Just then, a young boy, around eighteen years old, got out of the car and started walking up to the house. Wearing a faded pair of jeans Lee bought in Orlando, a Royal Thunder t-shirt Crys had gotten at a show in Ybor with Alice, and my old messenger bag slung over his left arm, he smiled at me beneath his buzz cut hair and those penetrating blue eyes. Smiling in return, I held up a battered little slip of paper and said, "Nice to meet you River," as he hugged me on the front porch, tears rolling down his face and lips curling into a smile.

SUGGESTED CLASS ROOM OR BOOK CLUB USE

DISCUSSION AND HOME WORK QUESTIONS

1. *Homecoming Queens* reveals many ways people, places, and narratives shape who we become. What are some ways social forces shaped the lives of the characters? What are some ways social forces may have shaped you or your loved ones?
2. Throughout the novel, the narrator reflects on the culture of Queens, a small town in the south. Think about your own expectations of small towns and the south, where do they come from and what might you be missing?
3. Queens is a fictional town built from elements of many small towns in the south. Discuss the ways Queens does or does not represent your own experiences in small towns, in the south, or more broadly in your life.
4. Many of the characters in this novel are deeply influenced by events earlier in their lives. Think about your own life, what are some major moments that may have shaped who you are?
5. The novel also shows different forms relationships and families can take in contemporary society. Think about and discuss what it was like reading about relationships and families that are not often pictured in contemporary media.

CREATIVE WRITING ASSIGNMENTS

1. Pick one of the characters in the novel, and move forward in time ten years. What is their life like, where do they live, and what do they do for a living? Compose a story that answers these questions.
2. Re-write the first chapter of the novel from Crystal's perspective.
3. Pick a character in the story, and write their story before, during, or after the events in the novel.
4. Beginning after the end of one of the last five chapters, write an alternative ending to the novel.

5. Pick a scene that the characters talk about in the book (i.e., some event you learn about in conversation, but do not witness with the narrator), and write that scene from the perspective of any character.

QUALITATIVE RESEARCH ACTIVITIES

1. Select any conversation or event in the book, and conduct a focus group to learn how other people interpret that conversation or event.
2. Select a character, and do a content analysis of that character. How do they talk? How do they see the world? What are their relationships (romantic, friendship, family, or otherwise) like? In what ways are they similar or different in relation to other characters? What information about them is missing and what information is presented in the novel? Overall, what can we learn from that character?

ABOUT THE AUTHOR

J. E. Sumerau, PhD, is the author of two prior novels exploring Queer experience in the south – *Cigarettes & Wine* and *Essence*. Alongside their fictional writing, they are also an assistant professor of sociology and the director of applied sociology at the University of Tampa. They are also the co-founder of the academic blog Write Where It Hurts (www.writewhereithurts.net), and a regular contributor to the academic blogs Conditionally Accepted at Insider Higher Ed (https://www.insidehighered.com/users/conditionally-accepted) and The Society for the Study of Symbolic Interaction Music Blog (https://sssimusic.wordpress.com). Their teaching, research, art and advocacy focuses on the intersections of sexualities, gender, religion, and health in the historical and interpersonal experiences of sexual, gender, and religious minorities, and has been published in numerous peer-reviewed academic journals and edited volumes. For more information on their research and other novels, please visit www.jsumerau.com.

CPSIA information can be obtained
at www.ICGtesting.com
Printed in the USA
LVOW13s1526270318
571329LV00005B/90/P